Zechariah

Get Back in the Game

Darrin Yeager

2024

Frames of Reference LLC

Zechariah
Get Back in the Game

Copyright © 2024 Darrin Yeager

All rights reserved. No part of this book may be reproduced in any form, known now or in the future, without written permission of the copyright owner, except for brief quotations in reviews or other materials.
https://www.dyeager.org/

ISBN 979-8-9889650-2-2
Published by Frames of Reference LLC

The integral sign with alpha and omega limits logo is a trademark of Frames of Reference LLC.
Unless otherwise noted, Bible passages are from the King James Version of the Bible.
Passages marked NKJV taken from the New King James Version of the Bible copyright ©1979, 1980, 1982 by Thomas Nelson Inc. Used by permission. All rights reserved.
Scripture quotations marked New Living Translation (NLT) are taken from the Holy Bible, New Living Translation, copyright © 1996. Used by permission of Tyndale House Publishers, Inc., Wheaton, Illinois 60189. All rights reserved.
31 27 09 20 03

Contents

Foreword	v
I Introduction	1
II What is The Matrix?	5
III The Matrix Guide to Christianity	7
IV The Problem: Abandoning the Commitment	13
V Haggai's First Message	21
VI Haggai: Temple Building	27
VII Problems Building the Temple	31
VIII Haggai's Second Message	33
IX Zechariah's Call to Repentance	35
X Haggai's Third Message	39
XI Haggai's Fourth Message	41
XII Zechariah's Visions	43
12.1 Rider on Horse	43
12.2 Four Horns and Four Craftsmen	50
12.3 Measuring Line of Jerusalem	51
12.4 High Priest and Satan	55
12.5 Lampstand and Olive Trees	58
12.6 Flying Scroll	63
12.7 Woman in Basket	64
12.8 Four Chariots	65

XIII Questions About Fasting	69
XIV Operational Pause	79
XV Zechariah: First Coming of Christ	89
XVI Zechariah: Second Coming of Christ	107
XVII The Problem	125
XVIII It's a Battle Out There	129
XIX The Opposition	135
19.1 The World	135
19.2 The Flesh	137
19.3 The Devil	138
XX Teamwork	139
XXI Why Do We Fail?	143
XXII Get in the Game	147
XXIII Strategy	153
23.1 The Scientific Method	153
23.2 Trust the Math	157
23.3 Seventy Weeks of Daniel	163
23.4 Didactic and Dialectic Thought	170
23.5 Post-Modern Philosophy	173
23.6 The Problem of Evil	176
23.7 That's Not What I Meant!	177
XXIV Conclusion	181
References	183

Foreword

WHEN DAD PASSED IT REMINDED me of the great teachers we've lost. Dad remains a giant of Christianity (though like many of the giants toiled in relative obscurity) and the more you knew him, the more you'll understand while he'll enjoy his promotion, we're deprived of more leadership than you can imagine. Besides dad passing, consider Walter Martin, the Chucks (Smith and Missler), and what each taught and warned about.

- Walter Martin — earnestly contend for the faith.
- Chuck Smith — teach the Word and reach the lost.
- Chuck Missler — science agrees with the God of the Bible.
- Dad — Don't divide over (his word) "fluff" issues.

You might not have heard dad's message, but I'd lost count of the times he said about something that's a fluff issue, it's not important (which doesn't mean a right or wrong answer doesn't exist though). We grew up in a Presbyterian church, attending others as well — some non-denominational, but over the decades everything from Baptist to charismatic.

I recall when Chuck Smith set up the tent in Costa Mesa dad wanted to know what was going on; he certainly had disagreement with Chuck on *at least* one area (those who know dad know *exactly* what that is), but in the end said Chuck was a good guy because what they didn't agree on was, well, fluff.

I always wondered how we could attend so many doctrinally different groups. It wasn't until years later dad related his "fluff" principal and I understood. Character, integrity, and accepting Jesus as savior mattered to dad, and frankly not much else. I could relate stories about dad's interaction with people he disagreed with (*strongly* if you know dad), but always considered friends.

Reading the problems existing in the Corinthian* (and today's) church, too much focus exists on non-important issues, choosing division over minor (sometimes non-doctrinal) issues instead of agreeing on the majors.

I've noticed each of our giants passed when what they were trying to teach the church desperately needed, but tried to ignore, and later openly rejected.

- Walter Martin — Walter's voice remains a stern warning against "modernizing" the church.
- Chuck Smith — Nobody wants to teach the Bible, and those that do … frequently ignore the lessons therein. Since Chuck's passing, Calvary Chapel unquestionably morphed from what he founded.
- Chuck Missler — Open hostility to science exists today, yet a stunning creation exists just waiting to be discovered.
- Dad — Fluff? That's now *most* important, even over the Gospel.

Examples abound for stupid, silly, and trivial ideas to divide over instead of focusing on the Gospel:

- At the dawn of the pandemic age (2020–2021) COVID and when/how the church meets (remote meeting via Internet doesn't count, it *must* be in person no matter what), basic sanitization, and protecting the flock from a pandemic (and banishing people not agreeing with certain political views).
- A friend related a story upon her first visit to a church they asked at the door if she was a Calvinist … for only Calvinists could fellowship there.
- Dad related a guy told him when he read the Bible, he would toss it back on the coffee table, but when he read the KJV, he reverently gently placed it down.

For myself, you wouldn't believe some of the hatred and gossip I've received over the years (most of it from "Christians" … atheists generally show more respect, at least to me) on many so-called vital issues Christians divide over — baptism, Calvinism vs free will, pre-trib, COVID, science, math, and other nonsense (i.e. "fluff"). It seems the church and its leadership forgot (or willfully cast aside) what Paul taught:

---

* See "The Troubled Church" ISBN 978-0-9831117-9-5 paperback and 978-0-9831117-7-1 ebook

> *Moreover, brethren, I declare unto you the gospel which I preached unto you, which also ye have received, and wherein ye stand; ... For I delivered unto you first of all that which I also received, how that Christ died for our sins according to the scriptures; And that he was buried, and that he rose again the third day according to the scriptures ...*

That's it. That's the Gospel. That's *the* definition of Christian. All else has (and always will be) ... fluff. If you agree on that (and the Bible is the inspired inerrant Word of God), we're together. Sadly, often in the church today you must be of political party "D" or "R", a Calvinist (or not), reject health protections in a pandemic, and other silly side issues having nothing to do with foundational doctrine — let's focus on the Gospel, not idiotic side issues.

A theory exists called Strauss–Howe generational theory, where societies traverse through four stages — the last being a crisis, as people forget the concepts and ideas from previous generations. At that point society either fixes the problems or sinks down in quagmire.

The church differs not. As great leaders of the church pass, the church faces its own fourth turning crisis, as lessons from those leaders are forgotten, or worse, willfully abandoned. At the dawn of the pandemic age (2020—2021) many pastors willfully and proudly abandoned rock-solid principles as the church enters its fourth-turning crisis.

The question: will the church and its pastors repent and return to foundational principles, or proudly continue down the path of hypocrisy, destroying their witness in the process?

Dad tried to warn us about the church dividing over stupid issues. I've seen that warning be both heeded, and sadly, ignored. We're repeating the mistakes of Judges as the great church leaders pass on.

> *In those days there was no king in Israel: every man did that which was right in his own eyes.* Judges 21:25

Putting that in today's terms:

> *In those days Christ was not king in the church: every pastor did that which was right in his own eyes.*

The only thing we learn from church history is the church fails to learn from history.

After someone passes, frequently discussion turns to how can we honor and respect them? What to put on the headstone, flowery words at the funeral, notices in the newspaper — all miss the mark. No, true honor is none of those. It's do you maintain their example, or ignore it? I'm with Elisha, I'd like a double-portion of what dad had.

> ...Elijah said unto Elisha, Ask what I shall do for thee, before I be taken away from thee.
> And Elisha said, I pray thee, let a double portion of thy spirit be upon me.   2 Kings 2:9

I've chosen to pick up dad's mantle, though it's likely as the church continues to focus on stupid and silly stuff few will choose ministry, fellowship, and friendship over politics. People simply don't want to listen and replaced fellowship with politics and litmus tests of fluff you *must* accept or be banished.

> ...we need to remember that we deal with individual people, not a class of students... people who have joy and sorrow, who hurt, who can be lonely, who can be happy, who can be involved or who can turn us off or tune us out.
> So what?
> Well, this means that we can not simply deliver material from the Bible, but that we must relate that material to Christ, to life ... and this must be done with real people in mind, with real life situations.   ~ James J Yeager, November 22 1971

I'll try dad to follow your example — hypocrisy is saying we're going to honor someone's legacy ... while ignoring his teaching and example. Why can't people just be honest?

- We want to take our church in a different direction; anyone not agreeing with new political positions will be asked to leave.
- We don't want to contend for the faith *once for all delivered to the saints* so we'll ignore warnings regarding "modernizing" the church.
- Science? We're anti-science so reject math, rational thinking, and logic.
- And we'll specifically focus (and divide over) fluff issues like politics and pandemics, and banish anyone holding different views, after all politics must have priority over ministry, the Gospel, and Paul's teaching.

It would be refreshing to see people be honest and admit they reject what they *claim* to follow. Dad's most important lesson? It's all fluff ... focus on 1 Corinthians 15. If you get that right, other minor points are just that. Minor.

...at 3 AM or any other time.

Statement of Faith

Most churches or groups have a "statement of faith" or "what we believe" document, and those may contain considerably more beyond the foundations of Christianity, sometimes wandering into political or theological stances which frankly hold little importance (i.e. those side issues are *Fluff*).

Statements of faith reveal the most important items in the group; if they contain stances on political issues, certain sins, or minor doctrine it demonstrates those are *the* most important above all else not listed.

Sadly, those can create division for the simple reason if a statement mentions one item but doesn't mention another, it's assumed the item mentioned holds more importance than the item not appearing therein. A modest proposal — reducing those lists and eliminating items not essential to Christianity; i.e. what you *must* believe to be a Christian, and little else.

For a statement of faith, what is the Gospel? And what defines Christianity?

- We don't care if you worship on Saturday or Sunday.
- We don't care what time you meet, if you meet in a building, or use virtual meetings.
- We don't care if you're a Democrat or Republican.
- We don't care if you're pre-trib, post-trib, or don't know what the tribulation is.
- We don't care if you're a Calvinist ... or not.
- We don't care what sin you've found yourself in (or continue to struggle with), and won't "rate" some sins as worse than others, as everyone is a sinner in need of God's grace.

Those are Fluff elements; these are not:

What We Believe

We believe in the "Four C's." If you accept those, we'll fellowship with you.

Condition
- For all have sinned, and come short of the glory of God (Romans 3:23)
- As it is written, There is none righteous, no, not one: There is none that understandeth, there is none that seeketh after God. (Romans 3:10–11)

⇒Everyone is a sinner in need of salvation.

Cure
- Moreover, brethren, I declare unto you the gospel which I preached unto you, which also ye have received, and wherein ye stand ... Christ died for our sins according to the scriptures; And that he was buried, and that he rose again the third day according to the scriptures (1 Corinthians 15:1,3–4)
- Neither is there salvation in any other: for there is none other name under heaven given among men, whereby we must be saved. (Acts 4:12)

⇒The Gospel isn't fluff or side issues; Jesus Christ's sacrifice is both necessary and sufficient for salvation.

Conclusive
- All scripture is given by inspiration of God, and is profitable for doctrine, for reproof, for correction, for instruction in righteousness (2 Timothy 3:16)

⇒The Bible is God's inerrant message to us. *All of it.* Claiming parts don't apply violates what Paul told Timothy — was Paul right or modern theology which contradicts what Paul said?

Commission
- I solemnly urge you in the presence of God and Christ Jesus, who will someday judge the living and the dead when he comes to set up his Kingdom: Preach the word of God. Be prepared, whether the time is favorable or not. Patiently correct, rebuke, and encourage your people with good teaching. For a time is coming when people will no longer listen to sound and wholesome teaching. They will follow their own desires and will look for teachers who will tell them whatever their itching ears want to hear. (2 Timothy 4:1–3 NLT)

⇒The church and individuals should teach and witness to others, and not chase the latest fads or winds of doctrine (political or theological). Popular opinion remains an atrocious strategy to run a church.

Conclusion
These boil down to:

1. You're a sinner and need Jesus as Savior.
2. The Bible is the inspired, inerrant Word of God, and we need to heed its message and teaching for life.
3. We need to teach *inside* the church, and witness to people *outside* it.

Note political opinions or disagreement over minor issues are all rocks better left unturned (if, that is, your mission is to profess the Gospel). Obviously many corollaries exist from those, but flow from the same basic principles.

- You can't witness to people if you hold a legalistic position making you appear loony ("You MUST meet IN PERSON on SUNDAY no matter what — or else").
- You can't witness to people if you hold a ridiculous anti-science position making you appear loony ("Don't put that potato salad back in the refrigerator, just trust the Lord you won't get sick if it sits out all day. Don't you have faith?").
- You can't "modernize" the church or the Bible, or ignore parts of it you don't like ("Paul didn't really write that." "That was only for their day and doesn't apply today." "This situation is different.").
- You can't rationalize and "pass the buck," saying when those previous errors occur, it's not your fault (or claim they won't destroy your witness, both outside *and* inside the church).

At the dawn of the pandemic age (circa 2020), many pastors and churches fell in to error and division over political ideas, adding to the long tradition of Christians dividing over unimportant issues; arriving at the essence of Christianity and the Gospel remains simple: you're a sinner, need Jesus Christ, and we're here to point the way.

Beyond that, everyone is welcome no matter their sin or minor doctrinal differences; removing or denigrating those not in agreement with fluff issues remains a significant error for pastors and church leadership (again, if the mission is to profess the Gospel).

Obviously, various doctrines do have correct answers (it's not possible for pre-trib *and* post-trib to both be correct). However, those minor doctrines (or non-doctrinal political issues) must be discussed in light of:

1. They're fluff and removing or defaming those disagreeing is wrong, and leadership *must* correct and rebuke any divisions arising from differences in fluff or when gossip arises (if the mission is the Gospel, not politics).
2. Everyone *must* be open to the idea they could be wrong, and listen respectfully (and discuss) opposing ideas; removing people disagreeing over fluff issues demonstrates serious errors in leadership.

The Gospel. It's really simple ... *Christians* make it hard.

CHAPTER I

Introduction

You are who you are and what you are because of what has gone into your mind. You can change who you are and what you are by changing what goes into your mind. ~ Zig Ziglar

MOTIVATIONAL SPEAKERS DON'T USUALLY impress me as many appear to be hucksters, packaging the same material over and over using different words to con people to purchase their wares. Yes, that's harsh, but frankly I don't care — as you'll discover, much of what people believe turns out to be false, and it's time for Christians to stop living in fantasy land. As John Loeffler says your failure to be informed doesn't make me a wacko.

However, I've listened to *one* guy over the years for one simple reason — he's absolutely right. Zig Ziglar. What does a motivational speaker have to do with your Christian life? We're glad you asked (or at least should have).

For far too long I've seen Christians slaughtered like pigs from a lack of preparedness when trials arrive, and I'm tired of watching. It's time to *do* something about it. If you're bringing (metaphorically) a knife to a gun-fight, you've only set yourself up as a pig proceeding to the slaughter (put that image firmly in your mind, because we'll come back to it. Often.).

So what about Zig? Read that quote again *You are who you are and what you are because of what has gone into your mind. You can change who you are and what you are by changing what goes into your mind.* To *some* extent, failing Christians result from poor teaching by their pastor, strange ideas about the enemy they face, false ideas about the God they serve, confusion over what Christianity is, uncertainty regarding the mission of the church, and a generally poor attitude.

If you want to change your ability to survive when reality throws a curve ball, you must focus on two things. First, change what goes into your mind, and second prepare for what awaits you.

Zig helps change your attitude, step one in transforming yourself from a 98-pound Christian weakling. But I doubt even Zig himself would claim he's much of a martial artist, thus arriving stage right, Chuck Norris. Sure, you've heard many famous Chuck Norris "facts" (like Chuck Norris is the reason Waldo is hiding), but you'll notice some traits of a well-trained martial artist such as confidence, humility, well-preparedness, and more, also appear as critical traits of the Christian life. That's no coincidence.

Some Christians might be disturbed about martial arts being associated with the Christian life. Fighting? Preparedness? Battle? Peace out, dude. Visualize whirled peas — here, have a flower. Why can't we just loooooove each other?

For the simple reason forces and powers exist that not only don't have your best interests at heart, they're out to destroy you, *and some of those exist in the church* (if you don't believe what you just read, study Jesus' parables in Matthew 13 and notice the birds lodging in the mustard tree are workers of Satan). If you're not ready and prepared, you'll suffer the fate of the pig (see, we told you that would come back). You must understand the reality of what faces you, *and* be prepared to defend against it. Fail either task and, well, you know what happens next (hint: it involves a pig).

This malady isn't a new trend, it's an old one. Way back in the Old Testament Israel faced similar problems. After one of their captivities, a few decided to return to the Holy Land and began to build the temple (the fact only a few returned hints of a problem, but we're ahead of ourselves). Naturally, some of their enemies began to attack, and at some point the Jews gave up and quit.

The battle's too hard, we're tired, let someone else do it (like the pastor), and so on. It's the *same* problem Christians face today, so we'll require the *same* solution Israel did.

Zechariah revealed future events (remember, the answers are *always* in the back of the book) to assist people in understanding exactly where they were going, and that the end was sure. It doesn't matter what it looks like now, it doesn't matter the odds, it doesn't matter what you're thinking — the end remains guaranteed.

For I know the thoughts that I think toward you, saith the Lord, thoughts of peace, and not of evil, to give you an expected end.
Jeremiah 29:11

Haggai was a different lot, writing a much shorter book containing a simple message — what are you guys doing slacking off? Haggai sounds like the stereotypical football coach motivating his team to stop being such slackers, and work harder. Be prepared, some of what you're going to hear isn't popular, or sometimes even pleasant (truth may not be). We'll uncover Israel's problem, and the solutions written by Zechariah and Haggai.

That's the historical view; we need to learn how we'll apply those lessons today (unless you like to be the pig) to transition from a 98-pound spiritual weakling to a seasoned, well-equipped Christian.

CHAPTER II

What is The Matrix?

BEFORE WE JUMP INTO THE MAIN PART OF the book, a brief movie examination will assist in understanding concepts we'll discuss later. "The Matrix" science fiction movie arrived in 1999, like other science fiction movies featuring a man-versus-machine plot, but this time with the machines holding the upper hand.

When the inevitable man versus machine war broke out, the machines depended on solar energy for power. It was believed darkening the sky would deny the machines their energy source, so people of the 22nd century create permanent storms to cripple solar energy. Like many ideas, it didn't work out exactly as planned, as the machines came up with a new solution to survive.

The human body creates heat and if that heat can be captured, it can be used to generate power. Building a pod to trap body heat and convert it to energy isn't difficult but getting people to stay inside *is*. Enter The Matrix. What is The Matrix? A computer-generated simulation of 1999 Earth designed to fool people into believing they actually live in reality, instead of a simulation inside a power plant; the machines designed The Matrix to hide reality and replace it with a phony and false idea people will readily accept, turning the human race into the Energizer bunny.

All except for our heroes. Morpheus escaped to rescue people from the deception of The Matrix, one being computer programmer Thomas Anderson, also known by his alias Neo. An important scene occurs when Neo meets Morpheus for the first time and Morpheus attempts to explain what Neo feels.

> MORPHEUS: *I see it in your eyes. You have the look of a man who accepts what he sees because he is expecting to wake up.*

> *Ironically, that's not far from the truth. ... Have you ever had a dream, Neo, that you were so sure was real? What if you were unable to wake from that dream? How would you know the difference between the dream world and the real world?*

Morpheus offers Neo a choice of two pills: one letting him wake up back in bed, and as Morpheus relates allows him to believe whatever he wants to about reality. The other pill provides Morpheus the ability to track Neo in The Matrix and rescue him. Neo decides to take a chance and be unplugged from The Matrix, and discover for the first time the real world.

Upon awaking, Neo has a difficult time accepting reality, as it's not easy to accept everything you think you knew turned out to be false and deceptive. Morpheus reminds Neo he never said it would be easy, all he offered was the truth. Over time Neo accepts and understands reality versus The Matrix, joining Morpheus in the fight against the machines.

Some people don't want to break free from fantasyland and live in the real world. They're comfortable in deception, and rather enjoy it — freedom can be hard and a struggle. The concept of preferring bondage, slavery, and deception over truth and reality isn't new — remember the Jews exiting Egypt? Oh, that we were back in Egypt, they grumbled; freedom can be tough, fantasyland remains comfortable, if fake.

The choice facing the Jews, the choice facing Neo, the choice you're facing right now: slavery and bondage or reality? Truth isn't always popular (or painless), and can't be found by a vote or popular opinion. As John Loeffler says, your failure to be informed (living in The Matrix) doesn't make me a wacko, and reality *always* votes last.

It's your choice, but we suggest it's time to get in the game.

CHAPTER III

The Matrix Guide to Christianity

YOU MAY HAVE SEEN THE TAG LINE ON our web site "Because it's 2:59 AM" and wondered where it came from; it stems from a political ad Hillary Clinton used in her bid for the Presidency.

> It's 3 AM and your children are safe and asleep. But there's a phone in the White House and it's ringing. Something's happening in the world. Your vote will decide who answers that call — whether it's someone who already knows the world's leaders, knows the military, someone tested and ready to lead in a dangerous world.
>
> It's 3 AM and your children are safe and asleep — who do you want answering the phone?

Hillary noted Obama had no real experience (while she did), and in the middle of the night you don't have advisers to lean on—you've got what you've got—so the person answering the White House phone *must* have experience. So how does a political ad relate to your Christian life?

For the Christian, *you* will answer the phone, not your pastor, friends, or anyone else. Are *you* prepared at 3 AM when nobody is around? At 3 AM, you've got what you've got. If you're depending on the availability of your pastor, friends, or even your husband or wife, you could be in for a *big* surprise when crunch time arrives, as it unquestionably will.

Yet you feel *something* is wrong with the world and what you're hearing — from politicians, friends, and yes, even pastors. Physicists inform us the world we inhabit contains at least ten dimensions, although we only experience four (three spatial dimensions plus time). What you see, touch, taste isn't actually the real world, and Peter reminds us it will all dissolve some day. In short, you're in The Matrix — an artificial system hiding the real world. To explain what you're feeling, you must break out of The Matrix.

Satan *wants* you to be comfortable in The Matrix, trapped in a church spending time on heresies and politics instead of truth, dividing over silly non-doctrinal issues, teaching potlucks instead of the Bible, sermonizing instead of line-by-line teaching, and thinking happy thoughts instead of providing practical applications of God's Word. Instead of being right, the church feels good about being wrong. The Matrix involves your *personal* life — the idea the Christian life is effortless, God makes life fun, with a Lexus, a pony, and ice cream!

Sorry folks, that's the system deceiving you *and* the church.

In the end, Christians fail because they're unprepared to face the challenges awaiting them — too many Christians live in The Matrix, having no concept of reality, replacing the sound doctrine of the Bible with The Matrix system of deception. Sadly, those living in The Matrix (including some "pastors") fail to recognize the state they're in.

Many Christians exist comfortably in their own deceptive Matrix — Hell doesn't actually exist so everyone is saved (universal salvation), it's the church's function to perform good works (social justice), the Bible must be reinterpreted for today (denying inerrancy), Satan doesn't actually exist (try opposing him for a while), and more. Those are The Matrix (or as Yoda would say "the dark side are these") — the system you're up against.

Just like the movie, many people living in The Matrix don't want to know the truth, and will fight to protect a false reality.

Just like Neo, you've got a choice to make.

1. Stop reading, ignore reality and believe whatever you want about your false "truths."
2. Study to find out what's truly going on, and see how deep the rabbit-hole goes.

If you're in the first group, stop reading right now and return to "I Love Lucy" reruns. Seriously. You'll be more comfortable (if in bondage), and you won't bother others preferring to live in reality.

For those in the second group, we're going to move on and assume you want to go beyond the basics. The absurdities of atheism, the lack of science in evolution, the deception of false gospels, and so on — those are *beginner* subjects. As Paul said, it's time to move beyond the milk and on to the meat.

Don't worry if you haven't mastered those subjects, we (and others) have written much on them and you can pick them up as we go along. As long as you're willing to logically examine what frequently has been sold unquestionably as true (and turns out to be completely false), you'll be fine.

But know this if you chose option two — people claiming to be Christians (yet trapped by a system deceiving them) might find the truth troubling, and just like the movie, will actively fight to preserve a false system they prefer over reality. Those are the people you're trying to rescue — don't be surprised if the deceived group includes pastors, teachers, and others.

For some of you, that will be difficult to accept, but when attempting to save a drowning person it's possible that person in their thrashing around will strike out at their rescuer. That's a hazard of the job you must be willing to live with.

> MORPHEUS: *I'm trying to free your mind, Neo. But I can only show you the door. You're the one that has to walk through it.*

Just because people call themselves Christians doesn't make it so (any more than calling yourself the President gets you a ride on Air Force One). The question you must ask — how much of Christianity can you reject and still claim to be a Christian? At what point does Christianity cease to be Christianity? Strangely, the correct answer comes from atheist Christopher Hitchens:

> *I would say that if you don't believe that Jesus of Nazareth was the Christ and Messiah, and that he rose again from the dead and by his sacrifice our sins are forgiven, you're really not in any meaningful sense a Christian.**

Truth comes from an atheist—having a superior understanding of Christian theology—rather than many "pastors." Those people inhabit The Matrix, the system you're up against. Be prepared to cast aside many things you've been taught that turn out to be false. No, we're not conspiracy theorists; we're interested in *truth*, not *popular* or *trendy*. People trapped by The Matrix fill the political, science, and popular opinion arenas. It's your responsibility to be different.

---

*   Sewell (2009)

Now that you've broken out of the system, do you want to help others? Obviously that's the right thing to do, as many of your brothers and sisters know nothing about the system they're living in, and require your help to break free from their bondage to join us in the real world. As a Christian, *you* must be prepared. Too many lazy Christians exist with no practical experience or knowledge, and when that 3 AM phone call comes in to their own house they fail to respond.

It's not enough to *know* what reality is—even Neo required training—you've must know *how to use what you know*, skills not widely disseminated. Some Christians may *know* what's true, they may even understand what the armor of God is, but they fail to train and prepare for the inevitable. Those people become ... well ... like the pig.

Morpheus told Neo a difference exists between *knowing* the path and *walking* the path. Knowledge by itself only explains why we're failing, it does nothing to prevent the problems. For that, you must take action on what you know — walk the talk. At 3 AM, you've got what you've got. Even once you escape The Matrix, that knowledge alone isn't sufficient. To be effective, you must know how to employ what you know.

What kind of Christian do you want to be? A prepared, well-equipped, well-trained veteran capable of rescuing your fellow Christians out of the sausage grinder, or a deluded Christian living in The Matrix where everything tastes like chicken?

It's time to put the uniform on and get (back) in the game. Sure, training isn't a lot of fun, but when you find yourself in the proverbial back-alley at 3 AM, you've got what you've got, and we're tired of seeing Christians lacking any spiritual tools at all, with the predictable result they end up failing spectacularly (read that as the metaphor being used throughout the book: slaughtered like a pig).

That *must* change. Sure, it's a new approach, but insanity comes from doing the same thing over and over yet expecting a different result (as Einstein said). You face a choice — right now, today, as you read.

- Stop reading and return to a phony and deceptive "reality" and believe whatever you want. You'll be comforted in bondage and slavery, but never truly be effective.

- Stay with us and together we'll explore how deep the rabbit-hole goes, because at 3 AM you've got what you've got ... and it's 2:59 AM.

As John Loeffler says, your failure to be informed does not make me a wacko, and reality *always* votes last. Just because you wish something won't make it true (only politically correct) — life isn't Disneyland where you wish upon a star and your dreams and fantasies come true.

MORPHEUS: *... all I'm offering is the truth. Nothing more.*

CHAPTER IV

The Problem: Abandoning the Commitment

THE FUTURE SEEMS TO BE AN OBSESSION with people. Glancing at supermarket tabloids near year's end you'll notice many focus on what they believe the future holds. Perhaps it's a fear of the unknown, or a desire to control the future, but man always attempts to predict tomorrow's events. Unfortunately, tabloids, palm-readers, fortune tellers, astrology, and other methods hold a dismal track record. Many "prophets" become celebrated if they're *half* right.

Moreover, anytime conflict flares up in the Middle East you'll find "experts" appearing on news channels answering one question: Is this the beginning of Armageddon? Will the Antichrist appear soon? Frequently the conversation becomes focused on one famous passage:

> *And that no man might buy or sell, save he that had the mark, or the name of the beast, or the number of his name. Here is wisdom. Let him that hath understanding count the number of the beast; for it is the number of a man; and his number is Six hundred threescore and six.* Revelation 13:17–18

Christians spend considerable time theorizing about the identity of this guy. Of course, it doesn't matter as the Antichrist can't be revealed until after the rapture of the church, but the church spends far too much time attempting to identify this man of sin. If you wander the Internet at all, you'll find many speculations; one of the more popular is Henry Kissinger, but others include Bill Gates, and even Barney the Purple Dinosaur. To show how easily virtually anyone's name equates to 666, consider the following about Barney — a joke appearing often on the Internet it doesn't seem to be possible to find an *original* source.

1. Start with the given: *CUTE PURPLE DINOSAUR*
2. Change all U's to V's: *CVTE PVRPLE DINOSAVR*
3. Extract all Roman Numerals: *C V V L D I V*
4. Convert into Arabic values: *100 5 5 50 500 1 5*
5. Add all the numbers: 666

Gasp! Barney is the Antichrist. Dastardly and fiendishly clever! No one will suspect a cute furry creature (Satan would have gotten away with it too, if it wasn't for those meddling kids!). Of course, that's absurd, but it does illustrate how crazy some of these ideas can be. In studies of Revelation many people obsess over the identity of the Antichrist, but it's not profitable for a few reasons:

1. We won't be here as he's not revealed until after the rapture.
2. It distracts (and takes time away) from other studies.
3. Playing games with numbers doesn't make sense — what does the number indicate? Are you using the correct formula? In Greek?

Don't spend too much time worrying about the identity of this guy. If you're ever trapped on a desert island with nothing else to do it might be an entertaining way to occupy your time, but that's about it. Even for prophecy buffs, more profitable uses of your time exist.

One book joins Revelation (and Daniel/Ezekiel as well) as the great prophetic books, but it doesn't receive much attention, simply because it's labeled a "minor prophet." Strange, as it gives a physical description of the Antichrist, and like Ezekiel details some rather advanced weaponry.

That book is Zechariah. While it's true the book details end time events, that's not its primary purpose. Rather, it's encouragement for God's people to leap off the sidelines and get back in the game. At various times God's people decided His work became too hard, so instead of pushing forward, they retreated.

Zechariah and Haggai were contemporaries, but while both wrote about the same situation, each approached it using different methods. Haggai wrote simply it's time to wake up and start moving, while Zechariah wrote of future events to encourage God's

ZECHARIAH

people to remain vigilant — while times may be tough currently, the end is sure, and the good guys win. Since both Zechariah and Haggai wrote about the same time, and the same events, their stories naturally intersect, and a proper study encompasses both.

Date	Year	Event
Aug 29, 520 BC	2nd year Darius, 6th month, 1st day	Haggai's first message (Haggai 1:1–11)
Sep 21, 520 BC	2nd year Darius, 6th month, 24th day	Temple building (Haggai 1:12–15)
Oct 17, 520 BC	2nd year Darius, 7th month, 21st day	Haggai's second message (Haggai 2:1–9)
Oct–Nov		Zechariah begins
Dec 18	9th month, 24th day	Haggai's third (2:10–19) and fourth (2:20–23) message
Feb 15, 519 BC	11th month, 24th day	Zechariah's night visions
Mar 12, 515 BC		Temple dedication (Ezra 6:15–18)
		Zechariah's final prophecies (9–14)

The situation was simple: in 539 BC the Jews obtained permission to return from captivity to Jerusalem and commence rebuilding the city and temple.

> *Now in the first year of Cyrus, king of Persia, so that the word of the Lord by the mouth of Jeremiah might be fulfilled, the Lord stirred up the spirit of Cyrus king of Persia, that he made a proclamation throughout all his kingdom, and put it also in writing, saying, Thus saith Cyrus king of Persia, The Lord God of heaven hath given me all the kingdoms of the earth; and he hath charged me to build him an house at Jerusalem, which is in Judah. Who is there among you of all his people? His God be with him, and let him go up to Jerusalem, which is in Judah, and build the house of the Lord God of Israel (he is the God) which is in Jerusalem.* Ezra 1:1–3

Cyrus allowed the Jews to return to Jerusalem. Only about 50,000 *did* return as many people preferred the sure conditions of captivity to the adventurous liberty of freedom*. It seems some people prefer the stability of bondage and slavery over freedom. When hearing of the small number who returned, we can't help but think of a quote attributed to Samuel Adams.

> *If ye love wealth greater than liberty, the tranquility of servitude greater than the animating contest for freedom, go home from us in peace. We seek not your counsel, nor your arms. Crouch down and lick the hand that feeds you; May your chains set lightly upon you, and may posterity forget that ye were our countrymen.*

If you're under attack or persecution, it might suggest you're a threat to the enemy. If you're in captivity, you're no threat. Nothing changed since Zechariah's time — it's time to get in the game. God's people should not retreat, they should be confident of the future and boldly progress forward.

Recall Israel in the wilderness after leaving Egypt as they cried to Moses "you brought us out here to die! Oh that we were back in Egypt!" Sure, the slavery thing wasn't so hot, but the food was yummy in the tummy! As long as they're taken care of, some people willingly trade freedom for slavery, a condition unchanged since the beginning of time.

The small group begins building the temple, but quickly runs into problems.

> *Now when the adversaries of Judah and Benjamin heard that the children of the captivity builded the temple unto the Lord God of Israel, then they came to Zerubbabel, and the heads of the fathers, and said unto them, Let us build with you; for we seek your God, as ye do, and we do sacrifice unto him since the days of Esar-haddon king of Assyria, who brought us here.*
>
> *But Zerubbabel, and Jeshua, and the rest of the heads of the fathers of Israel, said unto them, Ye have nothing to do with us to build an house unto our God; but we ourselves together will build unto the Lord God of Israel, as king Cyrus the king of Persia hath commanded us.*
>
> *Then the people of the land weakened the hands of the people of Judah, and troubled them in building, And hired counselors*

---

*   Ezra 2:64–65 — Some say 42,000, others 50,000. Ezra lists 42,360 Jews plus 7,500 others. The total depends on whether you include the servants and others in the total

against them, to frustrate their purpose, all the days of Cyrus king of Persia, even until the reign of Darius king of Persia.
Ezra 4:1–5

In the face of opposition and problems, they fold like a cheap lawn chair. At this point our heroes enter the scene, stage right; both Zechariah and Haggai arrive to encourage the people, but using different methods.

- Haggai encourages people by giving them practical advice.
- Zechariah encourages people by revealing God's plans.

The people quit working on the temple due to problems they faced, lack of dedication, or lack of knowledge of God's plan. For some reason, they failed to believe God's assurance. Once again, nothing has changed from the beginning of time, and we fail to learn the lessons history provides us. Fast forward to Jesus' time, as He and the disciples find themselves on the shore, and Jesus says "let's go to the other side." Give the disciples credit, they followed directions ... sort of. Upon setting out, they quickly find themselves in trouble (just like the Jews rebuilding the temple in Zechariah's day). They cry out to Jesus (waking Him up), proclaiming "don't you care we're dying out here!"

Ever feel like that? Here I am, trying to follow God's direction, and whammo! Problems arise. As we've noted, nothing has changed from the beginning of time. It happened in Zechariah's time, it happened in Jesus' time, and it happens today. But we're not done with the disciples yet — they wake Jesus up complaining they're about to perish, and Jesus looks around and simply says "be still" to the raging sea. The lesson comes as Jesus continues, asking them why did they doubt? Why did they have no faith? It's common to hear the faith they lacked was not fully understanding who Jesus was. But that's not true, for the simple reason they woke Him up. They *knew* He had the ability to handle the situation.

No, the faith they lacked was faith in Jesus' plan. When Jesus said "let's go to the other side," that's exactly what He meant — He did not say we're going to die in the middle of the lake. The disciples made the same mistake we often do, and it's a simple one. They didn't hear what Jesus said.

Jesus said "let's go to the other side," but they heard it would be an easy cruise to the other side. Jesus' words guaranteed arriving at the other side, but made no statement regarding the difficulty of the trip, nor what condition they would arrive in at the other side. It's a simple lesson — don't read more (or less) into God's Word. He means what He says and says what He means. With that, let's return to Israel's problems.

Zechariah means "Jehovah Remembers." Perhaps as you experience trials you think God forgets you. Much like the disciples in the boat, we forget the Lord says we'll go to the other side. Perhaps the biggest myth Satan wants you to believe is you're all alone. Nobody can relate, the situation is hopeless; even the apostle Paul felt depressed at times.

> *For we would not, brethren, have you ignorant of our trouble which came to us in Asia, that we were pressed out of measure, above strength, insomuch that we despaired even of life.*
> 2 Corinthians 1:8

Paul despaired of life? Yep. A passage easily misunderstood. Paul wasn't depressed, as the word "despaired" comes from Strong's Number G1820; in the Greek ἐξαπορέω (exaporeō), occurring 2 times in 2 verses in the New Testament, having more of a flavor of hopelessness or frustration in the current situation.

You can imagine Paul, Jeremiah, Isaiah, or any of the disciples and prophets being in despair. After all, they're sent to stiffnecked people who refuse to heed (or even listen to) God's Word. That's despair — when you hold the truth and people willfully reject it.

Where is the other verse this word occurs? Later in the same letter, Paul writes:

> *We are troubled on every side, yet not distressed; we are perplexed, but not in despair*
> 2 Corinthians 4:8

Another myth is people believing Christians don't suffer from those problems. Not true either. If a giant of the New Testament experienced those problems, you can rest assured you're not alone either, as even a casual reading of the Bible presents many situations where people are distressed and discouraged. It's not just one time when the Jews return to Jerusalem and halt building the temple, nor is it only Paul.

Elijah became depressed, afraid, and prideful immediately after his incredible experience on Mount Carmel, cowering in fear, and flees. Later in the Bible it reminds us Elijah was a guy like us, so if you've experienced any depression, fear, or pride, you're not alone — Elijah shared those feelings.

Most Christians have heard of the "hall of faith" in Hebrews 11. But you might have missed later in the chapter as it relates other heroes stoned, sawn in two, slain with the sword, and more. Just like me, you may think! Oh nobody knows the trouble I've seen! Hebrews adds a parenthetical thought "of whom the world was not worthy." You *must* understand your earthly circumstances bear no relation to your heavenly status or reward. God has His plan, and you can be confident it *will* occur, so always remember Romans 8:28 and its promise "all things work together for good to them that love God." We want to hear we'll *understand* all things, but that's not what the verse says.

Of course, one guy creates the prototype for bad news, what some say is the oldest book in the Bible: Job. The book does *not* give the answer we all want — why do people suffer. Let's take a glimpse and see what answer it *does* provide.

> *Now there was a day when the sons of God came to present themselves before the Lord, and Satan came also among them. And the Lord said unto Satan, From where comest thou? Then Satan answered the Lord, and said, From going to and fro in the earth, and from walking up and down in it.*
>
> *And the Lord said unto Satan, Hast thou considered my servant Job, that there is none like him in the earth, a perfect and an upright man, one that feareth God, and shunneth evil?*
>
> *Then Satan answered the Lord, and said, Doth Job fear God for nothing? Hast not thou made an hedge about him, and about his house, and about all that he hath on every side? Thou hast blessed the work of his hands, and his substance is increased in the land. But put forth thine hand now, and touch all that he hath, and he will curse thee to thy face.*
>
> *And the Lord said unto Satan, Behold, all that he hath is in thy power; only upon himself put not forth thine hand. So Satan went forth from the presence of the Lord.* Job 1:6–12

Here's Job, minding his own business when he gets hit with all kinds of trouble — without the benefit of knowing what we know, the events in heaven of chapter 1. Next his sons and daughters perish, along with livestock and virtually everything else. He loses his health next. One thing spared from this disaster — his wife. Of course, her remarkable advice was "Do you still hold fast to your integrity? Curse God and die!"

All that occurs in the first two chapters. Think it can't get worse? His "friends" show up, and for 35 chapters or so provide useless advice. Finally, we arrive at the real answer.

> *Where wast thou when I laid the foundations of the earth? Declare, if thou hast understanding. Who hath laid the measures thereof, if thou knowest? Or who hath stretched the line upon it? Whereupon are the foundations thereof fastened? Or who laid the corner stone thereof?* Job 38:4–6

In short, that means He's God, you're not. Sometimes the Lord lets you in on the secret, other times not. Haggai and Zechariah both encourage the people, but Zechariah provides a glimpse to how the end works out. Just like Revelation, the answers are in the back of the book — true also in the Old Testament. The message of Zechariah and Haggai remains as relevant — and simple — today as it was thousands of years ago:

Get back in the game!

CHAPTER V

Haggai's First Message

WHAT WENT WRONG? The people began building the temple, but encountered problems and quit. Haggai appeared in the middle of Zechariah's ministry and provided several short messages to motivate the people. In contrast to Zechariah, Haggai's message isn't focused on the sure end of events, rather it focuses on the heart and attitude of the people; some of what he has to say might not be comfortable.

> *In the second year of Darius the king, in the sixth month, in the first day of the month, came the word of the Lord by Haggai the prophet unto Zerubbabel the son of Shealtiel, governor of Judah, and to Joshua the son of Josedech, the high priest.* Haggai 1:1

Haggai wrote to both government and religious leaders. Immediately some people shout "you right-wing Bible-thumping fundamentalists, you're trying to force your religion on us." It's not about forming a theocracy, but the foundations of government should be based on Godly principles. It's simply a matter of using absolute standards to guide principles, and the only standard comes from the Word of God. If the government be Godly, it's because the people demand it, and if it slouches toward Gomorrah, it's because the people allow it.

> *Thus speaketh the Lord of hosts, saying: This people say, The time is not come, the time that the Lord's house should be built.* Haggai 1:2

They reached this conclusion from the opposition they faced building the temple. If it's a bit rough, that must indicate the Lord doesn't want us to continue. It *may* be the Lord closing the door when you're in trouble, it *may* be you're facing stiff resistance and should continue. You can't quit whenever trouble arrives, but you also can't be like the Church Lady finding Satan behind every crisis, stubbornly refusing to reconsider the situation. Trials and opposition while doing the Lord's work could be a sign He wants you to move on to something else, and it could be you're on the right track and the enemy wants you to quit.

How do you tell the difference? Prayer, reflection, counsel. No magic formula exists, so don't look for one. In this case, the Jews took opposition wrongly as a sign to quit, or they simply didn't want to work anymore. Instead, they turned to their own houses, and left the Lord's in ruin.

> *Then came the word of the Lord by Haggai the prophet, saying, Is it time for you, O ye, to dwell in your paneled houses, and this house lie waste?* Haggai 1:3–4

Paneled houses means not just completed, but lavishly decorated; they completely abandoned building the temple and went on with their lives. It's not wrong to take care of your house as you require a place to live. It's not even wrong to address your housing before building the temple.

The problem became one of priorities. Once the people completed adequate housing, it was time to turn to building the temple. Instead, they continued furnishing their homes, and ignored the Lord.

> *Now therefore thus saith the Lord of hosts: Consider your ways.* Haggai 1:5

The Lord through Haggai interrupts their lives, and reminds them to consider what they're doing. It's always a wise idea to pause and reflect on where you're at, and where you're going. As we see with the churches in Revelation many had the opposite view of their actual situation — those thinking they were doing fine the Lord tells them they're in trouble, while those struggling and worried about their situation the Lord says they're in good shape.

If you noticed their perception was opposite reality, you've earned a gold star. Today the same problem exists — many people thinking they're okay with "the man upstairs" should reconsider, while many struggling and worrying about their sin are in constant communion with God, and aren't in as bad a situation as they believe.

> *Ye have sown much, and bring in little; ye eat, but ye have not enough; ye drink, but ye are not filled with drink; ye clothe you, but there is none warm; and he that earneth wages earneth wages to put it into a bag with holes. Thus saith the Lord of hosts: Consider your ways.* Haggai 1:6-7

Haggai details a few of their problems. It seems no matter how much they sow, they don't harvest much. Working harder isn't the problem, rather it's the Lord trying to get their attention. Later the Lord will specifically state it was He who caused these issues.

Those wanting more and more will never be satisfied. How much is enough? Just a little bit more. It's common to rationalize your desire for "just a bit more" as reasonable, yet greed isn't just for the cigar smoking super rich, it's something even the lowest wage earners experience — that may be a shock for some people who think certain groups can't be greedy because they don't have much.

Not so. Some of the most greedy, covetous people appear in the lowest incomes. How can you tell if greed creeps in? Are you content, or not? Do you need just a little bit more? And when you receive a raise, still think just a little bit more? That's greed.

Paul said "Not that I speak in regard to need, for I have learned in whatever state I am, to be content (Philippians 4:11)." Does that describe you? Or are you trying to rationalize your desire for more? That's the key. You may have a little, or a lot, but be content with it (it's not the amount). That's hard to do because you'll rationalize you need just a bit more.

As a society, we continually seek more and more. If you saw the movie "Supersize Me" about a guy living completely on McDonald's food for 30 days, the movie revealed how large "small" portions have become, as today's small was previously considered large. Do you really need 64 ounces of soda in that extra-large big gulp? Maybe you missed the movie (it's worth watching), let's consider the expansion of home sizes over time.

> *Over the last 42 years, the average new US house has increased in size by more than 1,000 square feet, from an average size*

of 1,660 square feet in 1973 (earliest year available from the Census Bureau) to 2,687 square feet...

Why do you need another 1,000 square feet? Is your family 60% larger than it was in 1970? Not likely. No, the reason we need such large houses comes from requiring a place to put all our stuff. That sounds like what Haggai spoke of thousands of years ago, does it not? The idea "every day in every way we're getting better and better" simply isn't true — those same problems Haggai warned about (focusing on yourself and ignoring the Lord's work) still create problems today.

Go up to the mountain, and bring wood, and build the house; and I will take pleasure in it, and I will be glorified, saith the Lord. Haggai 1:8

Get moving! Haggai reminds them of three things.

1. Get off the couch.
2. Gather the supplies.
3. Get to work.

Who does Haggai direct the message to? It's for the people, not the leaders. If the people lead, the leaders will follow.

Christianity isn't a spectator sport, we all have work to do. God provides each Christian a special gift, and if you're not using it the church isn't functioning at peak ability. Too many Christians have the mistaken idea it's the pastor's job. Negative. It's time for *you* to get back in the game, as the pastor's function isn't to do the work, it's his task to train the people.

It's surprising this issue still pops up, perhaps because we don't study the Bible much anymore. For students of the Bible, this issue arose early in the church, and was settled. In Acts chapter 6, the disciples faced a similar situation as they performed most of the work. They conclude they should not abandon the study of God's Word, and instead appoint men of good character, while they themselves "will give ourselves continually to prayer, and to the ministry of the word."

That's as it should be. Pastors should study, minister, counsel, and perhaps most importantly, seek out and develop the gifts of

---

* https://www.aei.org/carpe-diem/new-us-homes-today-are-1000-square-feet-larger-than-in-1973-and-living-space-per-person-has-nearly-doubled/

the body of Christ. It's not the pastor's duty to do the work, it's his assignment to train the people who will do the work. Sadly, many churches don't function because we've raised a generation of lazy people. Perhaps you've heard of the 80/20 rule, meaning 80% of the work gets done by 20% of the people. Sometimes it could be 90/10, or even 95/5 — a situation certain to create burnout of your pastor and others doing the job.

> *Ye looked for much, and, lo, it came to little; and when ye brought it home, I did blow upon it. Why? saith the Lord of hosts. Because of mine house that is waste, and ye run every man unto his own house. Therefore the heavens over you withhold the dew, and the earth withholds her fruit. And I called for a drought upon the land, and upon the mountains, and upon the grain, and upon the new wine, and upon the oil, and upon that which the ground bringeth forth, and upon men, and upon cattle, and upon all the labor of the hands.*
> Haggai 1:9-11

Is He getting your attention? The Lord specifies it's not bad luck or anything else ... HE did it. The more you attempt to acquire "stuff," the less you'll be satisfied. How can I be so sure? We already have experimental evidence from a guy you might have heard of — Solomon.

> *I made for myself great works, I built myself houses, and planted myself vineyards. I made myself gardens and orchards, and I planted all kinds of fruit trees in them. I made myself water pools from which to water the growing trees of the grove. I acquired male and female servants, and had servants born in my house. Yes, I had greater possessions of herds and flocks than all who were in Jerusalem before me. I also gathered for myself silver and gold and the special treasures of kings and of the provinces. I acquired male and female singers, the delights of the sons of men, and musical instruments of all kinds.*
>
> *So I became great and excelled more than all who were before me in Jerusalem. Also my wisdom remained with me. Whatever my eyes desired I did not keep from them. I did not withhold my heart from any pleasure, For my heart rejoiced in all my labor; And this was my reward from all my labor.*
>
> *Then I looked on all the works that my hands had done and on the labor in which I had toiled; And indeed all was vanity*

and grasping for the wind. There was no profit under the sun.
Ecclesiastes 2:4-11

How much is enough? Whatever you've got be content. In the United States we buy things we don't need, with money we don't have, to impress people we don't like. Of course, no better example of that exists than Christmas, where even for a large portion of the church the season has little to do with the birth of Christ.

As Solomon would say, vanity, and grasping for the wind.

CHAPTER VI

Haggai: Temple Building

HAGGAI'S FIRST MESSAGE OBTAINED THE DESIRED effect, they returned to working on the temple.

> *Then Zerubbabel the son of Shealtiel, and Joshua the son of Josedech, the high priest, with all the remnant of the people, obeyed the voice of the Lord their God, and the words of Haggai the prophet, as the Lord their God had sent him, and the people did fear before the Lord.* Haggai 1:12

Notice again, both government and religious leaders receive the message. Not promoting theocracy (those generally don't turn out well) but leaders must be guided by Godly principles. It's a simple matter of when something crosses your desk, does it align with God or not? Not forcing religion on anyone, but murder remains wrong *because the Bible says so.*

A huge debate exists regarding the Christian founding of the United States. Interestingly, that debate only started in the 1950's, as before that nobody questioned what everyone knew. Perhaps you haven't read many Supreme Court decisions (they're generally surprisingly effortless to read, much easier than your phone bill); old decisions contain nuggets many people don't talk about.

> *But, beyond all these matters, no purpose of action against religion can be imputed to any legislation, state or national, because **this is a religious people**. This is historically true. From the discovery of this continent to the present hour, there is a single voice making this affirmation.*

If we examine the constitutions of the various states, we find in them a constant recognition of religious obligations. Every Constitution of every one of the forty-four states contains language which, either directly or by clear implication, recognizes a profound reverence for religion, and an assumption that its influence in all human affairs is essential to the wellbeing of the community.

... These, and many other matters which might be noticed, add a volume of unofficial declarations to the mass of organic utterances that **this is a Christian nation.**

SCOTUS: Church of the Holy Trinity v. United States, 1892

We are a religious people whose institutions presuppose a Supreme Being. We guarantee the freedom to worship as one chooses. We make room for as wide a variety of beliefs and creeds *as the spiritual needs of man deem necessary. We sponsor an attitude on the part of government that shows no partiality to any one group and that lets each flourish according to the zeal of its adherents and the appeal of its dogma. When the state encourages religious instruction or cooperates with religious authorities by adjusting the schedule of public events to sectarian needs, it follows the best of our traditions.*

SCOTUS: Zorach v. Clauson, 1952

As a side note, those Christians seeking to declare the United States under a theocracy are equally in error as those wishing to deny the religious heritage of the country. Theocracies generally don't end well, easily descending into tyranny. Religious freedom means religious freedom for everyone.

Adequate references exist in constitutions, laws, court rulings, and so on; the idea atheists desire of stomping out all religious truths from our past remains nothing more than historical revisionism.

That's not the problem (so we'll leave the founding of the country alone), atheists will always exist who fear God. Haggai solves the problem by providing the government with a morality standard. With no absolute morality, it's rule by majority, as atheism has no basis for morality. Read that carefully, it does *not* suggest atheists are immoral, or can't *be* moral, it *does* state they have no *basis* for their morality.

The problem of atheism and morality isn't a new one; you might have heard of Richard Dawkins (he's one of the leading proponents of atheism, and you might have heard an atheist recommending his books), and in an interview once was asked about where atheists obtain their ideas of right and wrong — morality.

> *There was an extended pause as Dawkins considered the question carefully. "Moral philosophic reasoning and a shifting zeitgeist." ...*
>
> *I asked an obvious question: "As we speak of this shifting zeitgeist, how are we to determine who's right"? ...*
>
> *"Yes, absolutely fascinating." His response was immediate. "What's to prevent us from saying Hitler wasn't right? I mean, that is a genuinely difficult question. But whatever [defines morality], it's not the Bible."**

Zeitgeist may be a term you haven't heard before, basically it means the spirit of the age — read that popular opinion, moral relativism, might makes right, and so on. It's not to say Dawkins actually meant Hitler *was* right, but using a shifting morality without absolutes, he can't say he wasn't as values change over time. A shifting zeitgeist could imply one hundred years from now history books will laud certain events condemned today. Why? Because the standard isn't absolute, it changes with popular opinion over time.

Thus, we're not advocating theocracy of any kind, but using an absolute standard for morality, not shifting value relativism, and the only absolute standard comes from the Word of God. If you're in government and not considering absolute morality, you've got problems.

> *Then spoke Haggai the Lord's messenger in the Lord's message unto the people, saying, I am with you, saith the Lord.*
> Haggai 1:13

Sometimes that's all we need, a reminder God is with us. Even a giant of the New Testament (Paul) needed occasional reminders. In Acts 18 Paul receives a vision not to be afraid but speak, for God is with him. Many times we're timid and afraid to speak, so the Lord reminds you, hey, I'm with you, what are you doing?

As John Loeffler says "I won't sit down, and I won't shut up; your failure to be informed does not make me a wacko." People are free to accept or reject whatever they desire, but too many

---

* Taunton (2007)

Christians keep silent. Paul wrote to Timothy to preach the Word and be ready in season or out of season. Unfortunately, many translations miss the implication of the Greek, as Walter Martin relates it actually means whether it's convenient or inconvenient.

That's not a license to be a jerk (using what I call "sandwich-board evangelism" — you know the type, standing on the corner with a sign saying The End is Near!), but timidity must go away. You still have free speech available to you, utilize it while you can.

> *And the Lord stirred up the spirit of Zerubbabel the son of Shealtiel, governor of Judah, and the spirit of Joshua the son of Josedech, the high priest, and the spirit of all the remnant of the people; and they came and did work in the house of the Lord of hosts, their God, In the four and twentieth day of the sixth month, in the second year of Darius the king.* Haggai 1:14-15

Once again, it's the people doing the work — it's not passed off to the pastor or government. One of the many problems with the social justice fad isn't only they replace the gospel with a false one (read that: heretical), but it replaces *your* responsibility to do God's work with the government. Where did the Bible ever say, sure, if you don't want to do it, pass off your responsibilities to someone else?

CHAPTER VII

Problems Building the Temple

YOU CAN GUARANTEE WHEN YOU GET INVOLVED and dive into the Lord's work, opposition won't be far behind. Just as the Jews began to build the temple, cue the creepy music as the evil guys enter stage left to thwart the work.

> *Now when the adversaries of Judah and Benjamin heard that the children of the captivity builded the temple unto the Lord God of Israel; Then they came to Zerubbabel, and the heads of the fathers, and said unto them, Let us build with you: for we seek your God, as ye do; and we do sacrifice unto him since the days of Esarhaddon king of Assyria, which brought us up here.*
>
> *But Zerubbabel, and Jeshua, and the rest of the heads of the fathers of Israel, said unto them, Ye have nothing to do with us to build an house unto our God; but we ourselves together will build unto the Lord God of Israel, as king Cyrus the king of Persia hath commanded us.*
>
> *Then the people of the land weakened the hands of the people of Judah, and troubled them in building, And hired counselors against them, to frustrate their purpose, all the days of Cyrus king of Persia, even until the reign of Darius king of Persia.*
>
> Ezra 4:1–5

To use the old cliche, when the going gets tough, the tough quit. Oops, that's not what it says, but that's frequently how it turns out. When difficulties arrive, will you reevaluate the situation, make corrections if required, and continue, or bail out and quit?

CHAPTER VII. PROBLEMS BUILDING THE TEMPLE

CHAPTER VIII

Haggai's Second Message

HAGGAI NOW MOVES TO PROBLEMS. The first message motivated them to return to the work, the last few deal with problems that frequently arise once you do begin. The first issue — some people always criticize, saying your efforts will amount to nothing.

> *In the seventh month, in the one and twentieth day of the month, came the word of the Lord by the prophet Haggai, saying, Speak now to Zerubbabel the son of Shealtiel, governor of Judah, and to Joshua the son of Josedech, the high priest, and to the residue of the people, saying, Who is left among you that saw this house in her first glory? And how do ye see it now? Is it not in your eyes in comparison of it as nothing?* Haggai 2:1–3

People like to compare what you're doing to what came before — Oy vey, I remember Solomon's temple, and this is no Solomon's temple. It's nothing. But God wants obedience, leave results to Him. Never forget who represents the biggest failure in the Bible. Noah. He built that boat in his driveway for decades, telling people judgment was coming. For all his effort, how many did he save? None. Zero. Zilch. A total failure.

But wait, there's more. When we arrive at the famous "hall of faith" in Hebrews 11, Noah makes an appearance. Why? God concerns Himself with character, not results. It's your responsibility to do what you're supposed to, it's God's task to obtain results from that effort.

> *Yet now be strong, O Zerubbabel, saith the Lord; and be strong, O Joshua, son of Josedech, the high priest; and be strong, all ye people of the land, saith the Lord, and work: for I am with you, saith the Lord of hosts.* Haggai 2:4

Do you think the message has changed? Paul in Ephesians 6:10 repeats the same idea with a command to be continually strong. It's not optional, it's something you need to do.

> *According to the word that I covenanted with you when ye came out of Egypt, so my spirit remaineth among you; fear ye not.*
>
> *For thus saith the Lord of hosts; Yet once, it is a little while, and I will shake the heavens, and the earth, and the sea, and the dry land; And I will shake all nations, and the desire of all nations shall come: and I will fill this house with glory, saith the Lord of hosts.* Haggai 2:5-7

Prophecy of the future, some of which we'll see in Zechariah, but much more in Revelation if you want to peek ahead. It's okay, the answers are always in the back of the book.

> *The silver is mine, and the gold is mine, saith the Lord of hosts.* Haggai 2:8

Many nations desire money and power, but the gold belongs to the Lord.

> *The glory of this latter house shall be greater than of the former, saith the Lord of hosts; and in this place will I give peace, saith the Lord of hosts.* Haggai 2:9

CHAPTER IX

Zechariah's Call to Repentance

ZECHARIAH BEGINS HIS BOOK WITH A CALL for repentance. Simply put, you require an attitude adjustment. To remind you what Zig Ziglar said, *You are who you are and what you are because of what has gone into your mind. You can change who you are and what you are by changing what goes into your mind.* You can make two mistakes, approach God with timidity (or fail to approach Him at all), or approach with a prideful attitude forgetting who you're addressing.

> *In the eighth month, in the second year of Darius, came the word of the Lord unto Zechariah, the son of Berechiah, the son of Iddo the prophet.*
> Zechariah 1:1

- Zechariah means "Jehovah remembers"
- Berechiah means "Jehovah will bless"
- Iddo means "approved time"

Put all those names together to read the Lord will remember, and bless, at the appointed time. You haven't been forgotten no matter how serious the storm looks right now, but are you (as the disciples were) still doubting and having little faith? When God says "let's go to the other side," do you have a problem believing you'll make it? Or perhaps you've heard something God *didn't* say: the cruise will be pleasant and smooth sailing.

> *The Lord hath been sorely displeased with your fathers.*
> Zechariah 1:2

They didn't do what they were supposed to. The Old Testament contains many examples of Israel failing to live up to their duty, but recall Paul wrote to Corinth these things were written for *our* admonition and learning. Don't let history repeat itself, rather break the mold and learn from history.

> *Therefore say thou unto them, Thus saith the Lord of hosts, Turn ye unto me, saith the Lord of hosts, and I will turn unto you, saith the Lord of hosts.* — Zechariah 1:3

You're never too far from the grace of God. Satan wants to convince you you're alone and God gave up on you, but the Bible contains many examples of the Lord calling back. Don't believe Satan's lies — you're not all alone as nobody ever travels so far God's grace can't find them, as Jesus said anyone coming to Him will not be cast away (John 6:37).

You can't mess up more than the grace of God can cover. That doesn't imply to sin so that grace may abound (as Paul noted in Romans), only don't ever think you're beyond God's grace and mercy — it's limitless. You need to repent, and that means a changed attitude. God knows the heart, and knows if you're trying to pull a fast one.

> *Be ye not as your fathers, unto whom the former prophets have cried, saying, Thus saith the Lord of hosts: Turn now from your evil ways, and from your evil doings; but they did not hear, nor hearken unto me, saith the Lord.* — Zechariah 1:4

Learn from the past, don't repeat it. Don't be stubborn. God sent prophets to Israel, but they refused to hear. Even Zechariah himself was killed in the temple he motivated them to build.

> *Your fathers, where are they? And the prophets, do they live for ever? But my words and my statutes, which I commanded my servants the prophets, did they not take hold of your fathers? And they returned and said, Like as the Lord of hosts thought to do unto us, according to our ways, and according to our doings, so hath he dealt with us.* — Zechariah 1:5–6

Don't listen to people who provide wrong ideas. Many ideas blow through the church and distract many. Some of those people even claim it's not actually in the Bible, but you should follow it anyway. A word exists for that kind of philosophy: heresy. Heretics in the church? Yep, and some of them could be pastors and write books, but their teaching comes not from the Bible one bit.

Ideas like collective salvation, where your salvation hinges on others. Does the New Testament contain any such idea? Of course not, it's an absurd notion. Your salvation depends on your acceptance or rejection of Jesus Christ. Nothing more. Another popular idea floating around surrounds the bizarre notion Hell doesn't exist, and in the end everyone will be saved. Really? What happened to the warning about blaspheming the Holy Spirit, and those who do will suffer *eternal* damnation?

People peddling such strange ideas live in the deceptive world of The Matrix. It matters not if they're "pastors," write popular books, pal around with politicians, or have PhD's behind their name. If they can't Biblically justify their ideas, it's only philosophy, not theology — and anyone claiming it's a Christian's duty to follow their non-Biblical ideas are at the least wildly uninformed (to be polite).

Before you can find encouragement, you've got to have a change of heart. The first few verses provide a reminder of what would be common to the Jews — they've refused to listen to the prophet's call to repent and turn back to God.

CHAPTER IX. ZECHARIAH'S CALL TO REPENTANCE

CHAPTER X

Haggai's Third Message

WE ARRIVE AT ANOTHER PROBLEM. Haggai's first message told the people they were distracted; his second, people complained it was nothing, and now the third saying if we built the temple God would bless us, and we still don't have a pony or ice cream. Haggai now reveals *why* the people weren't blessed, even though they appeared to be following God's instruction.

> *In the four and twentieth day of the ninth month, in the second year of Darius, came the word of the Lord by Haggai the prophet, saying, Thus saith the Lord of hosts: Ask now the priests concerning the law, saying, If one bear holy flesh in the skirt of his garment, and with his skirt do touch bread, or pottage, or wine, or oil, or any food, shall it be holy? And the priests answered and said, No.* Haggai 2:10–12

Holiness isn't transferable as holiness is the absence of uncleanness, sin, evil and so on. That may sound like splitting a definition, but it's not. Consider light and dark; if you've ever been in a totally dark cave you understand that dark (as a measurable quantity) doesn't exist. Rather, once you eliminate all light, you're in the dark. You can't add "dark" and make it so, you must extinguish the light.

Holiness works the same way. It's the absence of sin, corruption, evil, and so on. God isn't Holy because He possesses some measurable quantity of holiness, rather the absence of any evil makes God pure and Holy. Thus you can't transfer holiness by touching it to something unholy.

> *Then said Haggai, If one that is unclean by a dead body touch any of these, shall it be unclean? And the priests answered and said, It shall be unclean.* Haggai 2:13

Uncleanness is a quantity, and can be transferred. During the swine flu outbreak in 2010, only a tiny fraction of kids attended school (even the healthy ones). Why? As any parent knew, when many people were sick it was best to keep kids home for a few days because their wellness couldn't be transferred, but someone else's virus sure could be.

> *Then answered Haggai, and said, So is this people, and so is this nation before me, saith the Lord; and so is every work of their hands; and that which they offer there is unclean.* Haggai 2:14

Being unclean means the works don't count as they're contaminated. It's not doing work God wants, it's the proper attitude; we're reminded by God *character matters*.

> *And now, I pray you, consider from this day and upward, from before a stone was laid upon a stone in the temple of the Lord; Since those days were, when one came to an heap of twenty measures, there were but ten; when one came to the wine-vat to draw out fifty vessels out of the press, there were but twenty. I smote you with blight and with mildew and with hail in all the labors of your hands; yet ye turned not to me, saith the Lord.* Haggai 2:15-17

No matter what, they won't turn to the Lord. It's not rotten luck, it's the Lord trying to get your attention. Once again, we must be careful. When bad things happen it *could* be Satan, it *could* be the Lord getting your attention, it *could* be your own stupidity. In this case, the Lord reveals it's Him trying to obtain the attention of the people.

> *Consider now from this day and upward, from the four and twentieth day of the ninth month, even from the day that the foundation of the Lord's temple was laid, consider it. Is the seed yet in the barn? Yea, as yet the vine, and the fig tree, and the pomegranate, and the olive tree, hath not brought forth; from this day will I bless you.* Haggai 2:18-19

If the attitude is correct, the Lord rewards. It's not the work or results God wants, but the attitude.

CHAPTER XI

Haggai's Fourth Message

HAGGAI'S FINAL MESSAGE INVOLVES A DIRECT word to Zerubbabel regarding both the end times, and a sign of the Messiah that won't be discovered until Jesus' birth.

> *And again the word of the Lord came unto Haggai in the four and twentieth day of the month, saying, Speak to Zerubbabel, governor of Judah, saying, I will shake the heavens and the earth; And I will overthrow the throne of kingdoms, and I will destroy the strength of the kingdoms of the nations; and I will overthrow the chariots, and those that ride in them; and the horses and their riders shall come down, every one by the sword of his brother.* Haggai 2:20–22

As we've seen already in Haggai's previous messages, this involves a prophetic future detailed in Revelation.

> *In that day, saith the Lord of hosts, will I take thee, O Zerubbabel, my servant, the son of Shealtiel, saith the Lord, and will make thee as a signet; for I have chosen thee, saith the Lord of hosts.* Haggai 2:23

Who appears in the linage of Jesus? Zerubbabel in Luke 3:27.

CHAPTER XI. HAGGAI'S FOURTH MESSAGE

CHAPTER XII

Zechariah's Visions

WE MOVE TO A SERIES OF VISIONS Zechariah experienced. Depending on how you divide them, Zechariah contains either eight or ten visions (we'll employ the more common eight vision division). It's vital to remember these visions all occurred in one night, and were visions not dreams, as he's awake during the complete sequence.

12.1 Rider on Horse

Upon the four and twentieth day of the eleventh month, which is the month Sebat, in the second year of Darius, came the word of the Lord unto Zechariah, the son of Berechiah, the son of Iddo the prophet.
Zechariah 1:7

In modern terms, 519 BC — after Haggai's messages and a few months after the beginning of Zechariah's ministry in October and November of the previous year. As we've noted, Zechariah and Haggai's ministries intertwine in assisting Israel to remain committed to the task.

I saw by night, and behold a man riding upon a red horse, and he stood among the myrtle trees that were in the bottom; and behind him were there red horses, sorrel, and white.
Zechariah 1:8

In case you wondered how we could say Zechariah experienced these as a vision (a kind of interactive movie, you might say) Zechariah says he *saw* by night — not a dream, but an interactive vision. He sees one leader, with three others. Sometimes when reading prophecy people become confused with who or what the prophet speaks of. People obtain their PhD's by writing on various theories, but many times no doubt exists for the simple reason the Bible explains elsewhere what the prophecy means. When that happens, those PhD's look foolish with their pages and pages of "scholarship."

For example, scholars claim Isaiah didn't write the book bearing his name. They call this idea the impressive-sounding name "Deutero-Isaiah Hypothesis," simply meaning two Isaiahs wrote the book. You can read page after page explaining what scholars believe are variations in vocabulary and style, differences they believe confirm more than one author.

Remember our foundation — when reading prophecy you don't need to guess or expound strange sounding theories, just read the text. For the Deutero-Isaiah hypothesis, the definitive answer to the authorship of Isaiah appears in the Gospel of John.

> *But though he had done so many miracles before them, yet they believed not on him; That the saying of Isaiah the prophet might be fulfilled, which he spoke, Lord, who hath believed our report? And to whom hath the arm of the Lord been revealed?*
> John 12:37–38

You'll recognize this as part of the famous Isaiah 53 passage. More importantly, Isaiah 53 appears in the second "half" of Isaiah, the part scholars claim a different author wrote. That's their guess, does it hold up? Keep reading in John.

> *He hath blinded their eyes, and hardened their heart; that they should not see with their eyes, nor understand with their heart, and be converted, and I should heal them. These things said Isaiah, when he saw his glory, and spoke of him.*
> John 12:40–41

That passage isn't as familiar to most people, but it comes from Isaiah 6:9–10, or what scholars call the first "half" of Isaiah. Notice we considered verses 37–38 in John, and 40–41. What appears in verse 39?

> *Therefore they could not believe, because that Isaiah said again...*
> John 12:39

What did John tell you? He quoted both "halves" of Isaiah, and *attributed them to Isaiah*. Who wrote Isaiah (all of it)? Isaiah. You've been spared reading pages of boring pseudo-scholarship from people who fail to read the book they're supposedly an expert on.

Instead, allow let the text speak for itself. In this first vision, who is the leader? We don't have to guess, as verse eleven tells us it's the Angel of the Lord, or Jesus. No volumes of pseudo-scholarship required, just read the text with an open mind.

> *Then said I, O my lord, what are these? And the angel that talked with me said unto me, I will show thee what these are.*
>
> Zechariah 1:9

Once again, we don't have to guess, as Zechariah asks, and receives an answer. Don't fall for people (even with titles after their names) supplying voluminous arguments. The simplest explanation is *usually* the best. In Physics we called the attempt to hide a lack of understanding with volume "hand-waving," as Richard Feynman said:

> *Feynman was once asked by a Caltech faculty member to explain why spin one-half particles obey Fermi-Dirac statistics. He gauged his audience perfectly and said "I'll prepare a freshman lecture on it." But a few days later he returned and said "You know, I couldn't do it. I couldn't reduce it to the freshman level. That means we really don't understand it."**

Beware people supplying volumes of bizarre arguments in an attempt to hide their foolishness. The simplest explanation (and one requiring the fewest new ideas) is *usually* the correct one. God certainly didn't want to lock away His truths so only a select few could understand. Most of the ideas in the Bible are child-like (not child-*ish*) — in other words you don't need years of study to understand them.

Take the text for what it says, don't attempt to "read" something else into it. The problem arises when people don't *like* what the text says. When rejecting the clear and obvious meaning of a section of the Bible, impressive sounding (but empty) theories like "Deutero-Isaiah Hypothesis" must replace common sense to fool people into thinking the obvious meaning isn't the real meaning.

This perversion doesn't happen much except with the Bible. If I wrote you a letter and expressed a desire to invite you over for dinner, would you then turn to your wife and say "what does he mean, is he talking about a football game?" Why not? Because

---

*   Feynman (1964, page xii)

the text clearly states an obvious meaning. But when the Bible expresses the same clarity—yet people don't want to accept it—they'll invent bizarre theories making no sense, usually using one of the following arguments (call these tactics of rebellion):

1. That section only applied in that time, the Bible must fit in with today's society so that part doesn't apply today.
2. The writer didn't mean "xyz" when he said "xyz" he actually meant "abc."
3. "xyz" represents an allegory for (insert long-winded and boring idea here).

Who gets to choose when the text means what it says, and when the text means something that doesn't actually exist in the text? In that case, you've watered down Christianity to nothing more than man-centered designer philosophy, robbing it of its position as the inerrant Word of God.

Hurry, hurry, hurry, step right up, now create your own designer religion! Just pick the parts of the Bible you like, and discard parts you don't! Get anything you want from your version of Christianity. Now you can create sects like:

- THE SWINGERS BIBLE — just ignore all those pesky parts on adultery. While you're at it, discard all the marriage stuff, it's so confining! Paul's warning about adultery and other problems was only cultural, it certainly doesn't apply today, so if it feels good, do it.
- BILL AND TED'S BIBLE — delete all the warnings on drugs. Excellent! Party on dude!

Wait a minute, you'll say, you can't just cast aside verses you don't like just because you want to cheat on your wife and use drugs. Exactly. So why do we allow various groups to chop up the Bible to suit them? Why do *they* get to select what Paul meant after rejecting the clear and obvious meaning?

> *And the man that stood among the myrtle trees answered and said, These are they whom the Lord hath sent to walk to and fro through the earth.* Zechariah 1:10

Satan walks to and fro as well. We are not alone — the spiritual world intertwines with our physical world, and those failing to recognize that truth suffer as a result. The four dimensions we inhabit exist as a subset of the eleven or more dimensions of reality. That's not some Star Trek fantasy, not only is it modern science, it appears in the Bible.

If you recall 2 Kings 6, you've seen the Bible proving the additional dimensionality we inhabit. Elisha reported to the King of Israel their enemies' plans. Naturally, the King of Syria wasn't thrilled when his plans were thwarted over and over. Thinking he has a spy in his inner circle, they reply it's not them, it's Elisha who knows what the King speaks in his bedroom!

Thus, the King says go capture this Elisha person, and the Syrian army surrounds Elisha one night. Waking up, Elisha's servant notices the Syrian army and wakes up Elisha in a panic. Elisha shakes it off, giving the servant the cryptic answer "they that are with us are more than they that are with them," which the servant can't make add up (even under new math), going back to Elisha to roust him out of bed again.

Elisha figures he'll never achieve any sleep, so he asks the Lord to let the servant in on the secret, and the servant sees an army of chariots surrounding them. Of course, they were there all along (Elisha knew it), but the servant didn't know; the spiritual realm exists all around you, whether you know it or not.

> *And they answered the angel of the Lord that stood among the myrtle trees, and said, We have walked to and fro through the earth, and, behold, all the earth sitteth still, and is at rest.*
> Zechariah 1:11

The earth exists basically at peace, except for one group of people. If you're a student of history, you know this is a rare event as a war almost always exists somewhere on the globe.

> *Then the angel of the Lord answered and said, O Lord of hosts, how long wilt thou not have mercy on Jerusalem and on the cities of Judah, against which thou hast had indignation these threescore and ten years?*
> Zechariah 1:12

The majority of people on the earth rest, while Jerusalem and the people do not. They hadn't been following God's commands, and were in captivity. God frequently used the enemies of Israel as His arm of judgment, and this time they're in captivity for seventy years. This might seem backward — the enemies of God are at peace, while God's people struggle. But you must observe the larger picture. Habakkuk wondered why justice wasn't coming, and the Lord let him in on the secret. Once he knew the Lord's plan, he responded that's not exactly what I had in mind, God!

Some question why evil exists, or cancer, or other things if a good God does. The simple answer: He's God, you're not. You need God's perspective, so refer to Job chapters 38 & 40 to see what happens when Job tries to question God. You don't see the whole picture, while God simultaneously sees the end from the beginning (and how it all works out), so why do you think you can question God? For the Israeli captives, seventy years is a *long* time. Many might think God forgot about them, or God doesn't exist, or if He does, He can't or won't care about them. But not so. God doesn't forget, and you're not alone.

> *And the Lord answered the angel that talked with me with good words and comforting words.*   Zechariah 1:13

God hasn't forgotten — but maybe you haven't been listening. When Jesus told His disciples "let's go to the other side of the lake," that's not exactly what they heard. What they heard was "let's go on a cruise to the other side," meaning the journey would be comfortable and painless.

That's why they panicked when the storm came up — they didn't understand what Jesus said, for Jesus never told them about the circumstances of their journey, only the end point. It's quite easy to read more into what God says than what's there, and when you do you'll respond exactly as the disciples did.

> *So the angel that talked with me said unto me, Cry thou, saying, Thus saith the Lord of hosts; I am jealous for Jerusalem and for Zion with a great jealousy.*   Zechariah 1:14

A principle laid out over and over in the Old Testament restated, in case any doubt remained about how the Lord feels about the Jews and Jerusalem. He hasn't forgotten, He hasn't abandoned, He hasn't replaced. A tragic heresy creeps in saying the church has replaced the Jews in God's plan, since they rejected their Messiah. When people try to sneak in bizarre ideas like this, ask them to Biblically justify their position. In this case, where does God say the church replaced Israel? Nowhere, thus their idea is at best a personal opinion, at worst outright heresy.

Much like the Deutero-Isaiah hypothesis covered earlier, those promoting the idea the church replaced Israel simply haven't read the book. In this case, the famous 70 weeks of Daniel reveal the

ZECHARIAH

prophecy involves Daniel's people (the Jews), and their Holy City (Jerusalem). Since the prophecy hasn't been fulfilled yet (the end of sin, etc), it's clear the Jews still have a place in God's plan, as another strange idea bites the dust.

> *I would like to call your attention to the fact that great prominence is given in each of the ten visions to these truths: (1) that God is not through with the nation Israel; and (2) when God says Israel and Judah and Jerusalem, He means exactly those geographic locations. ... If you could persuade me that He is going to be unfaithful to the nation Israel, then I do not know on what basis I could believe that He is going to be faithful to the church.**

Take your Bible as it says without getting "scholarly" and you'll be much better off. We'll discover in a later section exactly *how* heretics deny Biblical truth (it's something called post-modern philosophy), but for our purposes, just remember to take the text as it says, so we can continue with Zechariah.

> *And I am very very much displeased with the nations that are at ease; for I was but a little displeased, and they helped forward the affliction.* Zechariah 1:15

As you travel through the Old Testament, you notice God uses the enemies of Israel as His arm of correction. In this case, those nations God used to correct the people went beyond the mission.

> *Therefore thus saith the Lord; I am returned to Jerusalem with mercies; my house shall be built in it, saith the Lord of hosts, and a line shall be stretched forth upon Jerusalem. Cry yet, saying, Thus saith the Lord of hosts; My cities through prosperity shall yet be spread abroad; and the Lord shall yet comfort Zion, and shall yet choose Jerusalem.* Zechariah 1:16-17

God hasn't forgotten about them. It may seem like a long time, but all things work together for good to those who love God, who are *the* called according to His purpose. Like Israel before, you might believe God forgot about you, or you're about to die like the disciples thought out on the lake. Sometimes you need character improvement, and sometimes what you need most you'll only obtain through trials and hard times. Character matters, so do yourself a favor and learn the lesson quickly, so you won't repeat it.

---

* McGee (1982, page 911)

12.2 Four Horns and Four Craftsmen

Some commentators treat this as two visions, others one. Since we're using Zechariah's visions divided into eight visions instead of ten, we'll treat this as a single vision. Don't worry about this or that division some scholar uses, after all those are the words of man and may or may not be correct.

> *Then lifted I up mine eyes, and saw, and behold four horns.*
> Zechariah 1:18

Horns represent strength. What are they? Once again (as you've learned by now), don't guess, keep reading as they'll be defined in the next verse.

> *And I said unto the angel that talked with me, What be these? And he answered me, These are the horns which have scattered Judah, Israel, and Jerusalem.*
> Zechariah 1:19

These powers and/or nations scattered Israel. Most commentators identify these with the four empires in Daniel (chapters 2,7,8), otherwise known as Babylon, Persia, Greece, and Rome. Daniel might be confusing, so the following chart might help identify what appears in Daniel's book.

Kingdom	Chapter 2	Chapter 7	Chapter 8
Babylon	Gold	Lion	
Medo-Persia	Silver	Bear	Ram
Greece	Bronze	Leopard	Goat
Rome	Iron	Beast	

The prophecies of Daniel in those three chapters agree with each other, and you'll also see them arise in Revelation.

> *And the Lord showed me four carpenters. Then said I, What come these to do? And he spoke, saying, These are the horns which have scattered Judah, so that no man did lift up his head; but these are come to terrify them, to cast out the horns of the nations, which lifted up their horn over the land of Judah to scatter it.*
> Zechariah 1:20-21

You don't pick on God's people, as you'll lose. Maybe not at first — it might even appear like you're getting away with it —

but justice *will* come. People become discouraged as they see evil prosper (just as Habakkuk did), but rest assured, evil *will* be judged, and at some point everyone will be accountable for their actions.

In this case, these four powers each become deposed themselves, with the exception of Rome that disintegrated from various internal corruptions ("The Decline and Fall of the Roman Empire" details it). As a side note, many of the problems in Rome face countries today, and since they fail to correct their mistakes they'll suffer the same fate as Rome. It seems the only lesson man learns from history is man learns nothing from history.

12.3 Measuring Line of Jerusalem

Zechariah continues his encouragement of the people as it's a glimpse of the future. Right now people have quit, but here's part of how it works out, so get back in the game. It's nice to remember the end, it may seem dark sometimes, but that doesn't mean it will always be. Like much of prophecy, this one contains both a near and far fulfillment; the remnant of Israel that returned needs to finish the temple, and yet it also looks to still future end-times.

> *I lifted up mine eyes again, and looked, and behold a man with a measuring line in his hand.* — Zechariah 2:1

What's going on here? Sometimes you may know, other times not. Many ask what the Bible means in a place, ignoring the simple advice that frequently these things are explained elsewhere in the Bible. Instead of engaging in those diversions, we'll just move to verse two.

> *Then said I, Where goest thou? And he said unto me, To measure Jerusalem, to see what is the breadth thereof, and what is the length thereof.* — Zechariah 2:2

You don't have to guess what this guy does, as the next verse tells you. Sometimes it's not the next verse, but the Bible frequently explains itself elsewhere, a fact many scholars miss when they guess what the Bible means (recall Deutero-Isaiah hypothesis, replacement theology, etc). Don't fall for the trap of "scholarship," simply read for yourself and see what the text plainly says.

> *And, behold, the angel that talked with me went forth, and another angel went out to meet him, And said unto him, Run, speak to this young man, saying, Jerusalem shall be inhabited as towns without walls for the multitude of men and cattle therein;*
> Zechariah 2:3–4

Walls exist for protection of the city. In ancient times without an air force or heavy artillery, tall and thick walls guaranteed an invading army could not penetrate the city. However, one problem remained — only a limited supply of food and water could be stored, thus the common tactic involved surrounding a city and simply waiting. Much like the children's staring game, it could take years to see who might blink first. Would the inhabitants of the city run out of food and water and starve, or would the army surrounding the city become tired and finally leave?

In the time Zechariah speaks of, not only will Jerusalem be so large due to all those living there, it won't have need of walls because of the next verse.

> *For I, saith the Lord, will be unto it a wall of fire round about, and will be the glory in the midst of it.*
> Zechariah 2:5

The Lord protects. That does *not* suggest failing in your preparations, as the horse is prepared for the day of battle, but safety is of the Lord (Proverbs 21:31). Two common mistakes occur. First, failing to prepare for what you reasonably expect will happen. Second, trusting in those preparations. It's prudent to prepare for what you see coming, but don't rely on yourself; recall the words of Isaiah:

> *But now thus saith the Lord that created thee, O Jacob, and he that formed thee, O Israel, Fear not: for I have redeemed thee, I have called thee by thy name; thou art mine. When thou passest through the waters, I will be with thee; and through the rivers, they shall not overflow thee; when thou walkest through the fire, thou shalt not be burned; neither shall the flame kindle upon thee.*
> Isaiah 43:1–2

Notice the text says *when* you pass through waters. If you've seen those little promise books in Christian bookstores you'll find lots of gooey stuff about love, but they'll miss in this world you *will* have tribulation. It's a sure thing. The promise is *when* those things happen you won't be abandoned.

The Lord protects; you can't die before your appointed time. That doesn't indicate you can walk in front of a freight train and not be severely injured — you'll quickly find out it was your appointed time (and a stupid idea at that) — Thou shalt not temp the Lord thy God. You have a specific duty to fulfill, and when it's done, it's time to move on, and your services are required elsewhere. But don't ask God to demonstrate His protection. That's a bad idea.

You'll notice through the Gospels Jesus avoided trouble when possible. If the creator of the universe avoided trouble when He could, should we mortals not do the same? Obviously yes. Some churches might use the end of Mark's Gospel to prove who the true Christians are — but again that's a bad idea. Mark 16 isn't a test of who the true Christians are, it's an example of the idea God watches over you.

At the end of Acts, Paul finds himself once again shipwrecked and on an island. When you're cold and tired, you first want to make a fire, which Paul set out to do by collecting wood, but he also collected a surprise — a venomous snake. When the snake latches on his arm the natives wait for Paul to keel over dead, but he doesn't. Paul shakes the snake off into the fire and keeps doing what he was doing. That's the idea behind Mark 16, not passing snakes around in stupid attempts to prove your true Christianity (I'd imagine groups doing such foolish things would have their groups stay rather small).

However, even if you don't see or feel the Lord's protection, that doesn't mean it's not there. Remember 2 Kings chapter 6 with Elisha and his servant. Elisha understood the Lord's protection existed even if he couldn't see it, but the servant didn't until it was revealed to him.

> *Ho, ho, come forth, and flee from the land of the north, saith the Lord; for I have spread you abroad as the four winds of the heaven, saith the Lord. Deliver thyself, O Zion, that dwellest with the daughter of Babylon. For thus saith the Lord of hosts: After the glory hath he sent me unto the nations which spoiled you; for he that toucheth you toucheth the apple of his eye.*
> Zechariah 2:6–8

Any time we see a flare-up in the Middle East, the only guarantee will be at some point Israel will be attacked. That piece of ground remains the apple of the Lord's eye, and history shows when enemies attack Israel, it doesn't matter the numbers, Israel survives. From Haman in Esther to Hitler and beyond, plots to eliminate the Jews always fail. We should remember the promises God made to Israel as we mess around in the Middle East. Verses like this should be plastered over the walls at the State Department as the old cliche about not being on the wrong side of history clearly applies in this situation.

Don't cozy up with the world either, as Peter says it will melt with fervent heat. Revelation refers to those who dwell on the earth — not just physically, but where your heart is. Be in the world, but not of it.

> *For, behold, I will shake mine hand upon them, and they shall be a spoil to their servants; and ye shall know that the Lord of hosts hath sent me.*   Zechariah 2:9

How much effort did the Lord expend? Shaking His hand. Recall the disciples in the boat with the storm. How much effort did Jesus expend? Jesus said "be still" and it was over, because the guy who created the sea controls it. What makes you any different from the disciples or Israel? During the storms of life, never forget who's in control. Just don't take that to imply life is painless, or "fair," because it certainly won't be.

> *Sing and rejoice, O daughter of Zion; for, lo, I come, and I will dwell in the midst of thee, saith the Lord.*   Zechariah 2:10

They quit building, so Zechariah provides a glimpse of the future when the Lord will dwell in their midst. In other words, don't give up the ship, it doesn't matter how desperate the situation looks right now, the end remains guaranteed.

We've also arrived at another strange idea as some groups endeavor to place themselves as Zion, or the 144,000 in Revelation. J Vernon McGee points out* when God says geography or people, it means exactly that. We can make *application* of these passages to our life, but don't change the *interpretation* to something other than what the text plainly says. Interpretation is right or wrong, but many applications might exist. Don't confuse the two.

The only way someone could apply sections like this to the church or other groups comes from denying the clear and obvious meaning in the text. If Israel doesn't mean Israel, who gets to decide what God's Word actually says? Christianity then becomes a designer religion, where each person takes whatever they want

---

*   McGee (1982, page 914–915)

and makes it whatever they want, with the absolute truth of the Bible disappearing.

> *And many nations shall be joined to the Lord in that day, and shall be my people: and I will dwell in the midst of thee, and thou shalt know that the Lord of hosts hath sent me unto thee. And the Lord shall inherit Judah his portion in the holy land, and shall choose Jerusalem again.* Zechariah 2:11–12

It looks bad right now, but know the future. We've covered this idea before, so we'll keep moving.

> *Be silent, O all flesh, before the Lord; for he is raised up out of his holy habitation.* Zechariah 2:13

Don't awake the sleeping bear, as the Lord defends a small parcel of ground called Jerusalem.

12.4 High Priest and Satan

> *And he showed me Joshua the high priest standing before the angel of the Lord, and Satan standing at his right hand to resist him.* Zechariah 3:1

This Joshua isn't the Joshua of the sixth book of the Bible, he's the High Priest. Who stands next to him doing what he always does? Satan always accuses. Zechariah saw Satan, so he's not some psychological mental problem — he's real.

Like many doctrines, one of two errors can be made regarding Satan. First, you can become too focused on him thinking he's behind every door, and every problem. Rest assured, if you spend all night in a bar, drink way too much, and then be arrested for drunk driving, you can't say the devil made me do it, it's your fault, and your responsibility.

Focusing on Satan too much becomes like an old Saturday Night Live skit with Dana Carvey as the church lady. If you remember the tag line from the skits, just about every one contained the phrase "could it be, perhaps SATAN?" Sadly that's a parody of what many believe — Satan lives around every corner.

The other problem comes as some believe Satan doesn't exist. Another dangerous idea, perhaps not as funny as the church lady, but just as serious an error. Satan isn't a metaphor for what we struggle with psychologically, he's a real being who doesn't have your best interests in mind. It's interesting to notice increasing interest in the supernatural and vampires on TV and movies, but when you get to the reality of Satan many people dismiss it.

That could be one of Satan's greatest deceptions — get people involved in the occult, but deny *his* existence. Dastardly clever.

> *And the Lord said unto Satan, The Lord rebuke thee, O Satan; even the Lord that hath chosen Jerusalem rebuke thee. Is not this a brand plucked out of the fire?* Zechariah 3:2

A strange phenomenon exists as some people think they can (or should) take on Satan themselves. That's not a good idea, as Satan's smarter than you are, has more experience, and likely knows more about the Bible than you do. The LORD rebukes Satan, not us. You shouldn't take him on yourself; Michael the archangel didn't directly engage him in Jude, rather declared the Lord rebuke you.

At this time Jerusalem lay in ruins — perhaps many thought the city could never be rebuilt. Here's another instance when you should note it matters not what the odds are, or what the current conditions are; when the Lord says it's going to be rebuilt, it will be rebuilt. When He says let's go here, you're going to make it.

> *Now Joshua was clothed with filthy garments, and stood before the angel.* Zechariah 3:3

The high priest appeared pretty striking from our perspective. From God's, not so much. Attempts to stand before God covered in your own belief of good works won't cut it; you have no hope of appearing righteous. Because of that, some people have problems believing they can't fix the terrible things they've done before they were Christians (or after). You're right, you can't, so we move to the next verse.

> *And he answered and spoke unto those that stood before him, saying, Take away the filthy garments from him. And unto him he said, Behold, I have caused thine iniquity to pass from thee, and I will clothe thee with change of raiment. And I said, Let them set a clean turban upon his head. So they set a clean turban upon his head, and clothed him with garments. And the angel of the Lord stood by.* Zechariah 3:4–5

Notice who does the cleaning. Not Joshua. *You* can't fix it; God removes the dirty clothes and provides you with new clean ones. A subtle danger creeps in when thinking your efforts contain some value, as if you're "helping" God along. Not really. Salvation remains a gift from God — you contribute *nothing*. Don't fall for the subtle mistake your works hold redemptive value. Of course, that doesn't imply you can live your life and party it up, because you can't. Rather, how someone lives their life reveals clues to their status.

> *And the angel of the Lord protested unto Joshua, saying, Thus saith the Lord of hosts; If thou wilt walk in my ways, and if thou wilt keep my charge, then thou shalt also judge my house, and shalt also keep my courts, and I will give thee places to walk among these that stand by.* Zechariah 3:6–7

You've been saved, since that's done by God in exchanging your dirty clothes. But do you want to be used? Then you must be a good representative. You must respond and follow directions. God doesn't force Himself on anyone. Even if you're saved, you don't *have* to do anything. Rest assured, the Lord will accomplish His work, but by using someone else with a willing heart (Esther 4). The *response* to the cleansing God provides is a desire to be obedient. It's not I'm saved since I'm doing all this stuff, it's I'm doing all this stuff because I want to. You never give up your ability to say no if you so wish.

At this point, how's the temple construction going? They quit. Zechariah's message: get back in the game. Don't despair, don't be discouraged. Sure, life can be tough, but don't quit. You will ultimately be successful.

> *Hear now, O Joshua the high priest, thou, and thy fellows that sit before thee; for they are men wondered at; for, behold, I will bring forth my servant the BRANCH.* Zechariah 3:8

The redeemer will arrive. Jesus. Notice in your Bible branch appears in all caps (or it should), as it's a title for Christ.

> *For behold the stone that I have laid before Joshua; upon one stone shall be seven eyes; behold, I will engrave the engraving thereof, saith the Lord of hosts, and I will remove the iniquity of that land in one day. In that day, saith the Lord of hosts, shall ye call every man his neighbor under the vine and under the fig tree.* Zechariah 3:9–10

The land may be polluted today, but some day it will be made right. Just like Joshua standing before the Lord with what appears to be nice clothes (but are soiled), the land itself suffers under bondage of corruption. It's not the way God intended it (or created it); someday the Lord will remove the iniquity of the land and restore it to what it should be.

12.5 Lampstand and Olive Trees

In the previous vision, God cleanses Joshua. Joshua now needs to understand what power he needs for his service, leading to one of the most famous verses in the Bible.

> *And the angel that talked with me came again, and waked me, as a man that is wakened out of his sleep,* Zechariah 4:1

Apparently Zechariah became a bit drowsy during these events; more proof he was awake.

> *And said unto me, What seest thou? And I said, I have looked, and behold a lampstand all of gold, with a bowl upon the top of it, and his seven lamps thereon, and seven pipes to the seven lamps, which are upon the top thereof,* Zechariah 4:2

Zechariah was a priest, and would think of the lampstand in the temple, but this one differed from the one in the temple as this lampstand never required filling with oil; it appeared to have its own system designed to keep it filled at all times. The priests had to continually create and supply the lampstand or it would go out, but the Lord supplies this lampstand Himself. Oil represents the Holy Spirit, once again that's not something you can obtain for yourself, but if you allow the Lord to perform the filling, you'll find it's a never-ending supply.

> *And two olive trees by it, one upon the right side of the bowl, and the other upon the left side thereof. So I answered and spoke to the angel that talked with me, saying, What are these, my lord?* Zechariah 4:3-4

Again confused, he asks.

> *Then the angel that talked with me answered and said unto me, Knowest thou not what these be? And I said, No, my lord.* Zechariah 4:5

The angel chastises him a bit, as he should have understood these symbols. Too many people shun prophecy or other sections of the Bible believing them too hard to understand. Not so. Not only did God provide His message in relatively clear terms, He holds us accountable to understand what He's told us.

The problem in the church today involves people who don't want to think or work for themselves, rather it's the pastor's job to figure everything out and then tell us. Unfortunately, when that 3 AM phone call comes, or you're stuck somewhere without a cell phone or other means of communication, you've got what you've got, and if you're not prepared you'll fail. It's *your* responsibility to dig in and understand.

> *Then he answered and spoke unto me, saying, This is the word of the Lord unto Zerubbabel, saying, Not by might, nor by power, but by my spirit, saith the Lord of hosts.* Zechariah 4:6

Recall the setup — the Jews began building the temple, but quit. Zerubbabel began the building, but after they encountered difficulty, abandoned the project. As we've noted before, that's why Zechariah and Haggai appear on the scene — get back in the game! It's a reminder to never forget what power actually accomplishes the task. It's not your finances, your Lexus, or your PhD. Once again, Zechariah's writing provides the encouragement by reminding them of the sure ending.

> *Back in the days of Zechariah there was a remnant that needed this encouragement because they were overwhelmed by opposition, and they were beset by doubts and by fears. So the vision was given—it is the Word of the Lord unto Zerubbabel—to encourage them.**

Working via your own skills, power, and money won't accomplish much. If you don't employ the weapons God provided, you're a casualty. Satan keeps us working in our own strength, and we fail. If we do things God's way, there's success. Why don't we?

> *Who art thou, O great mountain? Before Zerubbabel thou shalt become a plain; and he shall bring forth the headstone thereof with shoutings, crying, Grace, grace unto it.* Zechariah 4:7

What did God just say? Not by power, nor by might, but by *My* spirit. Do you see a mountain of opposition in your way? If you allow God to use His power (and not rely on yourself) those

---
*   McGee (1982, page 924)

mountains become a plain. Recall the disciples in the boat with Jesus during the storm. When Jesus wakes up, how much effort did He expend? Two words proved sufficient to end the storm, and the same guy from the boat can flatten the mountains of opposition as well.

Do mountains exist in our lives? Perhaps you're staring at a mountain, wondering how you'll get past it. Perhaps like Paul and others, you're discouraged. Maybe you see no possible way to overcome and make it to the other side. If so, you're missing a critical example from Physics called Quantum Tunneling. Simply put, a particle lacking in energy somehow finds itself on the other side of a quantum barrier.

That might not be clear — or even interesting — so let's provide a more familiar example. Suppose a seven month old baby is just beginning to play ball (it's never too early to toss the 'ol pigskin around). His mother and father give him a bowling ball (16 pounds), take him to Mount Shasta and say have at it boy, roll the ball up and over the mountain. If you were placing bets, would you bet he could do it?

Did you see the "Back to the Future" movies? You might remember Doc and his plans, but Marty had problems understanding the concepts. Doc said "you're not thinking fourth dimensionally Marty" to which Marty replies, "Yeah, doc, I've got problems with that." You're in the same boat if you would bet against — you're not thinking quantum mechanically.

Somehow (against the odds and what we plainly see) we find the ball on the other side of the mountain ... the mountain became a plain before the Lord. Once again what lays before us isn't what the Lord sees, and what we think of as mountains in life are nothing but plains to God.

An interesting Bible study is to find all the phrases "but God" in the Bible — it appears over 40 times (Genesis 31:7, 48:21, 50:20, 1 Samuel 23:14, Psalm 73:26, Acts 7:9, Romans 5:8, Ephesians 2:4, Philippians 2:27, etc). You'll quickly discover how we view things frequently looks like a mountain, but to the Lord it's all flat land. Those verses may show a situation hopeless and futile, *but God*.

Yeah, that applies to other people, but my situation is different. I've got a *really* big mountain, so this doesn't apply to me. Chuck Missler says never underestimate a person's ability to rationalize, so yes, it *does* apply to you, in your situation. Paul told us in Ephesians to "be strong in the Lord and in the power of His might

(Ephesians 6:10)," a verse in the present imperative voice; it's a command to be continuously strong.

> *Moreover the word of the Lord came unto me, saying, The hands of Zerubbabel have laid the foundation of this house; his hands shall also finish it; and thou shalt know that the Lord of hosts hath sent me unto you.* Zechariah 4:8–9

It may seem bleak now, but it will be finished, and Zerubbabel will be the one finishing it. Sometimes you won't see the result of your work, sometimes you will. In this case, Zerubbabel needed special motivation to get back in the game, with the Lord telling him he *will* finish the temple, so don't quit. In fact, as the Lord says, this is a prophecy of a future event, and when it comes true you'll *know* it was the word of the Lord.

> *And if thou say in thine heart, How shall we know the word which the Lord hath not spoken? When a prophet speaketh in the name of the Lord, if the thing follow not, nor come to pass, that is the thing which the Lord hath not spoken, but the prophet hath spoken it presumptuously; thou shalt not be afraid of him.* Deuteronomy 18:21-22

Prophecy authenticates. It's not difficult to spoof miracles (remember Moses verses Pharaoh in Egypt as the magicians duplicated Moses' miracles ... up to a point), but telling the future authenticates God as God. Peter lived with Jesus, ate with Jesus, and lived with Him for years. Yet in his letter even he doesn't rely on what he saw, but states we have the more sure word of prophecy. For example, Daniel's 70 weeks predicted the exact day Jesus would present Himself as Messiah.

Don't rely on emotion, as it can fool you at 3 AM; your emotions, experiences, and the physical world around us can all be used to fool you. Don't count on them, stand on what Peter said, the sure word of prophecy as it authenticates the remainder of the Bible. That's how you know all those promises about not leaving you are true.

> *For who hath despised the day of small things? For they shall rejoice, and shall see the plummet in the hand of Zerubbabel with those seven; they are the eyes of the Lord, which run to and fro through the whole earth.* Zechariah 4:10

The plumb line assists building, in its simplest form it's a rock on a string held up revealing vertical so walls are built vertical. Day of small things? Go big or go home is the slogan ("super size me"), but the Lord says don't despise the small things. Recall Elijah after Mount Carmel in 1 Kings 19. Immediately after a tremendous victory from the Lord the next chapter finds Elijah:

- Afraid (1 Kings 19:3)
- Depressed (1 Kings 19:4)
- Pouting and Prideful (1 Kings 19:10)

Elijah becomes fearful, depressed, desires to end his life, and prideful. What does the Lord do? After the wind, earthquake and fire, he hears a small voice, one of the Lord. And the voice said to Elijah, "What doest thou here, Elijah?" To restate, get back in the game! Elijah was a man like us. Do we get afraid, frustrated, and prideful?

Recall another instance of to and fro in the Bible from 2 Chronicles 16:9 "For the eyes of the LORD run to and fro throughout the whole earth, to show Himself strong on behalf of those whose heart is loyal to Him." Go back and read that, it's actually a rebuke of the King who didn't rely on the Lord, but instead counted on his Lexus and resources to save the day.

Frustrated as work starts and never ends? The Lord says to Zerubbabel the work has been started, and you'll see it finished. When you receive a vision for a project, but it gets tough, sometimes the Lord lets you in on the secret, that you'll see the end. Get back in the game, as it's not by might, nor by power, but by His spirit. Don't attempt to use your own resources.

> *Then answered I, and said unto him, What are these two olive trees upon the right side of the lampstand and upon the left side thereof? And I answered again, and said unto him, What be these two olive branches which through the two golden pipes empty the golden oil out of themselves? And he answered me and said, Knowest thou not what these be? And I said, No, my lord.* — Zechariah 4:11–13

Zechariah should have understood what he saw, but didn't. But he did ask, and receives an answer.

> *Then said he, These are the two anointed ones, that stand by the Lord of the whole earth.* — Zechariah 4:14

Who are these guys? Lots of speculation, but they don't say, so we won't guess. Many believe they're the two witnesses in Revelation, others have different views. Since the Bible doesn't specify, we apparently don't need to know.

12.6 Flying Scroll

Now the visions turn from comfort to warnings as the Bible comforts the afflicted, and afflicts the comfortable.

> *Then I turned, and lifted up mine eyes, and looked, and behold a flying scroll. And he said unto me, What seest thou? And I answered, I see a flying scroll; the length thereof is twenty cubits, and the breadth thereof ten cubits.* Zechariah 5:1-2

A cubit being about 18 inches, the scroll measures roughly thirty feet by fifteen feet. If you believe nothing in the Bible appears by accident, the size of ten cubits by twenty cubits equals the Holy place of the tabernacle and the Porch of Solomon in the temple* (Exodus 26:15-25 for tabernacle dimensions and 1 Kings 6:3 for dimensions of Solomon's porch). Zechariah would recognize the size as a priest.

> *Then said he unto me, This is the curse that goeth forth over the face of the whole earth; for every one that stealeth shall be cut off as on this side according to it; and every one that sweareth shall be cut off as on that side according to it.* Zechariah 5:3

Two parts to the law exist, laws regarding your relationship with God, and laws regarding your relationship with man. People think they're getting by with it because God hasn't judged them... yet.

> *I will bring it forth, saith the Lord of hosts, and it shall enter into the house of the thief, and into the house of him that sweareth falsely by my name; and it shall remain in the midst of his house, and shall consume it with the timber thereof and the stones thereof.* Zechariah 5:4

The law came so you would understand your sin and know your guilt before God. It doesn't bring redemption, but a curse as your works don't save, rather they demonstrate your lack of savability. It's a warning you're not getting by with it. Don't mistake God's patience for approval.

---

* McGee (1982, page 926)

12.7 Woman in Basket

> *Then the angel that talked with me went forth, and said unto me, Lift up now thine eyes, and see what is this that goeth forth. And I said, What is it? And he said, This is an ephah that goeth forth. He said moreover, This is their resemblance through all the earth.*
> Zechariah 5:5–6

Some translations write ephah instead of basket. How much is an ephah? About ten omers. That helps a lot, doesn't it? Okay, in terms most of us understand it's roughly six or seven gallons.

> *And, behold, there was lifted up a talent of lead; and this is a woman that sitteth in the midst of the ephah. And he said, This is wickedness. And he cast it into the midst of the ephah; and he cast the weight of lead upon the mouth thereof. Then lifted I up mine eyes, and looked, and, behold, there came out two women, and the wind was in their wings; for they had wings like the wings of a stork, and they lifted up the ephah between the earth and the heaven.*
>
> *Then said I to the angel that talked with me, Where do these bear the ephah?*
>
> *And he said unto me, To build it an house in the land of Shinar; and it shall be established, and set there upon her own base.*
> Zechariah 5:7–11

Shinar is a name for Babylon. In Revelation 17 mystery Babylon is destroyed (false religious system), and in Revelation 18 the commercial Babylon is destroyed. Israel began as an agrarian society, but in captivity in Babylon became commercialized. In this vision that commercial attitude returns to Babylon, ultimately for judgment in Revelation 17 and 18.

Some prophecies you find in the Bible describe the destruction of Babylon that some commentators believe already happened. But those prophecies say Babylon will never be inhabited again (Isaiah 13:19–20), so it's still yet future. Some things become clear just by reading your Bible, a stunningly obvious step many people never take.

More people are familiar with Revelation than Zechariah, but the strange idea prophecy has already been fulfilled remains a popular deception, as it can be popular to dismiss Revelation as an allegorical book and not real, or as events already occurred —

fulfilled prophecy. Wait a minute, you're telling me we've already seen the following from Revelation:

- Hail and fire mixed with blood, a third of trees burned up, and all the grass (Revelation 8:7)
- One-third of the sea becoming blood (Revelation 8:8)
- One-third of sea life, and one-third of ships (Revelation 8:9)
- One-third of people die (Revelation 9:15)

Yeah, we've seen all that. Right. Revelation obviously hasn't occurred yet, anyone claiming so either hasn't read the book, doesn't understand English, or just doesn't want to believe what's in black and white. Two reasons why not to be shocked at such strange ideas:

1. Truth doesn't care.
2. People are free to believe whatever they want.

As John Loeffler says, reality always votes last. It matters not if nobody or everybody believes something, it only matters if it's *true*, and truth isn't a popularity contest.

12.8 Four Chariots

And I turned, and lifted up mine eyes, and looked, and, behold, there came four chariots out from between two mountains; and the mountains were mountains of bronze.   Zechariah 6:1

Bronze symbolizes judgment — the serpent on a bronze pole (Exodus 21:9), the bronze altar (Exodus 27:2), etc; this vision involves judgment.

In the first chariot were red horses; and in the second chariot black horses; And in the third chariot white horses; and in the fourth chariot dappled and bay horses.   Zechariah 6:2-3

What do these mean? You could guess, or you could note the Bible uses idioms consistently (the principle of expositional constancy) and compare Revelation 6:

- red = war
- black = famine, inflation
- white = false peace
- dappled = death (pale green, chloros)

If you want to dig into it, read Revelation 6.

> *Then I answered and said unto the angel that talked with me, What are these, my lord? And the angel answered and said unto me, These are the four spirits of the heavens, which go forth from standing before the Lord of all the earth.*
>
> Zechariah 6:4–5

So what do we make of this? Once again, you don't need a PhD thesis to understand, just read on in Revelation for the explanation.

> *The black horses which are therein go forth into the north country; and the white go forth after them; and the dappled go forth toward the south country. And the bay went forth, and sought to go that they might walk to and fro through the earth; and he said, Go from here, walk to and fro through the earth. So they walked to and fro through the earth. Then cried he upon me, and spoke unto me, saying, Behold, these that go toward the north country have quieted my spirit in the north country.*
>
> Zechariah 6:6–8

If you want all the detail, read Revelation as your homework. To finalize the prophetic visions, allow Jon Courson to summarize.

> *Prophetically, Zechariah's vision tells the story of Israel. In 1948, when she was brought back home again, the Lord was in the midst of the myrtle trees once again (1:7–11). The powers that came against her ended up being "hammered" themselves (1:8–21). In 1967, Jerusalem was "measured" when the city was brought under the Israeli flag (2:1–5). Like Joshua, Israel will see that she has need of being cleansed and robed by the blood of Jesus Christ (3:1–5). When that happens in the time of the Tribulation, her light will shine brightly (4:2–5). But, as seen in the flying scroll, those who do not acknowledge the reality of the redemptive work of Jesus Christ will be judged for their sins (5:1–4). The commercial systems that manipulate and rip people off will be done away with (5:5–11), replaced by righteousness when, following the judgment of the Tribulation, Jesus rules and reigns from Jerusalem (6:1–8).**

That concludes the visions; the rest of the chapter is *not* a vision, it's something Zechariah actually performed, as the Lord gives him a strange assignment.

---

* Courson (2006, page 898)

ZECHARIAH

And the word of the Lord came unto me, saying, Take of them of the captivity, even of Heldai, of Tobijah, and of Jedaiah, which are come from Babylon, and come thou the same day, and go into the house of Josiah the son of Zephaniah; Zechariah 6:9-10

"Then" means after the previous 8 visions, as Zechariah receives an assignment from the Lord.

Then take silver and gold, and make crowns, and set them upon the head of Joshua the son of Josedech, the high priest;
Zechariah 6:11

Mixing royal kingship and priesthood? Not a good idea as 2 Chronicles 26 relates Uzziah the King trying to mix royal and priestly duties, with not such good results. It's separation of powers.

But when he was strong, his heart was lifted up to his destruction; for he transgressed against the Lord his God, and went into the temple of the Lord to burn incense upon the altar of incense. And Azariah the priest went in after him, and with him fourscore priests of the Lord, that were valiant men: And they withstood Uzziah the king, and said unto him, It appertaineth not unto thee, Uzziah, to burn incense unto the Lord, but to the priests the sons of Aaron, that are consecrated to burn incense. Go out of the sanctuary; for thou hast trespassed; neither shall it be for thine honor from the Lord God.

Then Uzziah was angry, and had a censer in his hand to burn incense; and while he was angry with the priests, the leprosy even rose up in his forehead before the priests in the house of the Lord, from beside the incense altar. 2 Chronicles 26:16-19

This assignment Zechariah receives is a bit strange; in case you missed the idea of a King and priest, the next verse should make it clear.

And speak unto him, saying, Thus speaketh the Lord of hosts, saying, Behold the man whose name is The BRANCH; and he shall grow up out of his place, and he shall build the temple of the Lord. Zechariah 6:12

BRANCH should be in all caps, it's a title of Jesus, just in case you missed the hint about a king and priest.

Even he shall build the temple of the Lord; and he shall bear the glory, and shall sit and rule upon his throne; and he shall be a priest upon his throne: and the counsel of peace shall be between them both. And the crowns shall be to Helem, and to Tobijah, and to Jedaiah, and to Hen the son of Zephaniah, for a memorial in the temple of the Lord. And they that are far off shall come and build in the temple of the Lord, and ye shall know that the Lord of hosts hath sent me unto you. And this shall come to pass, if ye will diligently obey the voice of the Lord your God. Zechariah 6:13–15

CHAPTER XIII

Questions About Fasting

THE NEXT TWO CHAPTERS OF ZECHARIAH involve questions regarding fasting and other rituals, revealing an interesting attitude of those asking the questions (which also still concern us today).

> *And it came to pass in the fourth year of king Darius, that the word of the Lord came unto Zechariah in the fourth day of the ninth month, even in Chisleu.*
> Zechariah 7:1

These questions arrive about two years after the visions of previous chapters as work on the temple proceeds.

> *When Bethel had sent unto the house of God Sherezer and Regem-melech, and their men, to pray before the Lord, And to speak unto the priests which were in the house of the Lord of hosts, and to the prophets, saying, Should I weep in the fifth month, separating myself, as I have done these so many years?*
> Zechariah 7:2-3

They mourned for the temple, but since it's being rebuilt, do we need to continue? It's a legitimate (if strange) question. Do you need to obtain an opinion whether you should pray for something or not? By asking the question they're not concerned about the issue itself, but the ritual.

We've come to the b-word — burnout. If you're working for the Lord, do you get tired? Some people say no, but that's not true. You *will* get tired sometimes, and you will need a rest. Service for God is tough, and you'll get tired. This body requires rest, and you're foolish not to give it some; if you over-rev an engine or keep it at too high an RPM for too long, it blows up. Never be ashamed or afraid to take a break, as the body (and mind) become frayed by continual expending of effort. It's not a question of *if* you need a break (as we all do), but *why*: is it a ritual you're doing from habit, or is it service for the Lord?

Service isn't a "got to," rather it's a "get to." You're never *forced* to work for the Lord, you're *allowed* to. That doesn't mean you won't be tired, and certainly doesn't mean you should never take a rest. It's okay to have a break, but check the attitude. If you're tired, yet motivated, that's good. If you're dreading your "ministry," perhaps it's time to re-evaluate.

Notice the air of pride creeping in — should I continue to separate myself? Legalism creeps in, another clue this might be a ritual only, and not service for the Lord. Are they desiring to appear in public as spiritual (if legalistic), or is this sincere expression? Many are more comfortable with legalism because under legalism it's trivial to check how you're doing.

- Read ten chapters in the Bible. Check
- Went to church Sunday *and* Wednesday. Check
- Helped a little old lady across the street. Check
- Witnessed to five people. Check

Thus, I'm good with God. It's the same attitude these guys had — we're fasting so we must be okay. It's a legalistic attitude, not a fellowship one. Is what you're doing good or bad? It's not the act, it's the attitude, and the answer contains three points:

1. Good attitude means fast is good.
2. Bad attitude means fast is bad (Isaiah 58).
3. Nothing changes God's plan (chapter 8).

Notice God didn't command this fast, God generally commands feasts. That doesn't mean fasting is bad, but don't let it become a ritual. Prayer and fasting isn't getting your way as if God grants wishes like a genie, it's aligning yourself with God's plan and enlisting for duty. You should make your requests to God, but like any father, sometimes the answer comes back no. Never view prayer and fasting as a magic tool to get your wishes (I want a pony! and ice cream too!).

God differs from pagan gods. Remember Elijah and Baal's servants on Mount Carmel as the prophet issues a challenge to the pagan followers. Let's set up an altar and have Baal's servants call on it, and I'll set up an altar and call upon the living God. The one who answers by sending fire shall be the true god.

Naturally, the servants of Baal didn't accomplish much (except making ruin of Elijah's altar), and at one point even cut themselves and screamed (1 Kings 18:28), the idea being god will hear and respond if we're in crisis. But no answer cometh. Finally, Elijah has a simple one-verse prayer, and God sends fire down and consumes the complete altar. God won't hear because of extreme behavior, you don't need to shout, and God doesn't grade by how many words you speak. It's attitude of the heart, not the method used. God doesn't need to hear many words, a simple and quiet request is all that is required.

> *Then came the word of the Lord of hosts unto me, saying, Speak unto all the people of the land, and to the priests, saying, When ye fasted and mourned in the fifth and seventh month, even those seventy years, did ye at all fast unto me, even to me?*
> Zechariah 7:4–5

A small group asked the question, but the response is to all the people. Did you do your service to God? Or as a ritual or something you just do out of habit? In your service *to* God, don't forget *about* God. In Revelation chapter 2, we should learn the lesson of Ephesus. Sure, they were dedicated about doctrine and such things, but in all their detail they forgot about God Himself.

It's attitude, not activity, God desires. Paul dealt with a similar issue — what about eating meat offered to idols? In 1 Corinthians 8:8 Paul writes it doesn't matter if you eat or not, your *attitude* matters. If you think eating meat is bad, it's bad, but if you recognize the idol means nothing and you can freely eat the meat, that's fine as well.

> *And when ye did eat, and when ye did drink, did not ye eat for yourselves, and drink for yourselves? Should ye not hear the words which the Lord hath cried by the former prophets, when Jerusalem was inhabited and in prosperity, and the cities thereof round about her, when men inhabited the south and the plain?*
> Zechariah 7:6–7

Instead of the current situation, why not listen to God in the first place? God didn't command this ritual, and you wouldn't be in this position if you paid attention to God originally; the captivity came from failure to follow God, so instead of fasting trying to fix the problem, why not avoid the problem in the first place?

Look back to 1 Samuel 15 as Saul didn't exactly follow God's command. He was told to utterly destroy all the sheep and cattle, but upon his return, Samuel greets him and Saul says he's followed all the word of the Lord. Samuel responds why then do I hear cattle and sheep? Saul explains he saved the best for a sacrifice.

Not a bad idea, except it didn't follow what the Lord directed. Samuel replies "Hath the Lord as great delight in burnt offerings and sacrifices, as in obeying the voice of the Lord? Behold, to obey is better than sacrifice (1 Samuel 15:22)." Following God's instructions results in superior outcomes. Don't avoid the instruction, and then fix the resulting problems later.

> *And the word of the Lord came unto Zechariah, saying, Thus speaketh the Lord of hosts, saying, Execute true judgment, and show mercy and compassions every man to his brother; And oppress not the widow, nor the fatherless, the sojourner, nor the poor; and let none of you imagine evil against his brother in your heart.* Zechariah 7:8–10

The command is for the people toward their fellow man. Don't think a fast makes you right with God when you're ignoring everything else.

> *But they refused to hearken, and pulled away the shoulder, and stopped their ears, that they should not hear.* Zechariah 7:11

"Pulled away the shoulder" — it's active refusal and rebellion. Like a child, sometimes you can put your hand on the shoulder and they get the message. But if they're in a pout and rebellion, they pull away in active defiance. You don't have to follow God, but don't be deceived in your rebellion God didn't mean what He said. It's popular today to deny the Bible says what it does; tactics of rebellion employ two main ideas:

1. That was for another time, the Bible needs to fit in with today's society so that part doesn't apply.
2. That doesn't really mean what it says, it's actually an allegory for...

People utilize those methods to call themselves "Christian," while denying any of God's law they don't want to follow; you can "prove" Jesus was a Republican (or Democrat if you wish), and nobody can show otherwise. Of course, that's a tongue-in-cheek idea, but the principle remains: those seeking to follow their own ideas instead of God's use those methods to deny whatever part of the Bible they wish to ignore. If you don't like the Bible, fine. It's your choice. But you look rather foolish claiming when it says one thing (and it's abundantly clear), it means something completely different. At least have the guts to say you reject the Bible, instead of trying to fudge some twisted meaning where none exists.

> *Yea, they made their hearts as an adamant stone, lest they should hear the law, and the words which the Lord of hosts hath sent in his spirit by the former prophets; therefore came a great wrath from the Lord of hosts.* Zechariah 7:12

Not only do they reject God's Word, they're stubborn and refuse to change. However, don't make the mistake stubbornness is *always* bad. Failure to listen to God's Word isn't good, but refusing to compromise and agree with those who "modernize" God's Word (changing the clear meaning or ignoring parts they don't like) isn't bad, or refusing to accept someones drug use as "something that works for them," instead of speaking the truth.

> *Therefore it is come to pass, that as he cried, and they would not hear; so they cried, and I would not hear, saith the Lord of hosts.* Zechariah 7:13

You won't listen to me, I'm not going to hear you. You can't treat God as a fire extinguisher "in case of emergency break glass" whenever you're in a bind. God looks for a relationship, but honors your free will choice to avoid Him. In that case, He will give you what you want — just don't expect to be able to call in a favor when you want it.

The Lord is not being mean, He gives you what you want. If you want life, love, peace, and joy, you can have it. If however you reject those ideas, God will give you exactly what you want. Some people complain about that (after all, all the opposite characteristics of God exist in a place called Hell), but what could be more reasonable than being pro-choice?

> *But I scattered them with a whirlwind among all the nations whom they knew not. Thus the land was desolate after them, that no man passed through nor returned; for they laid the pleasant land desolate.* Zechariah 7:14

The land laid like that for a loooong time; it wasn't prime real estate for thousands of years. The only reason people want it now is because the Jews have it, and if you have a pulse you've discovered certain groups have a hatred for the Jews. If you've heard of "replacement theology" with the church replacing Israel, and the Jews aren't God's people anymore, or modern Israel isn't actually Israel, those people have a tough time with the rest of Zechariah, as God makes clear the Jews have a future destiny.

Well, if you hold the theory that God is through with Israel, you can't handle the Book of Zechariah. My friend, Zechariah makes it clear that God is not through with Jerusalem and He's not though with the nation Israel.*

We won't delve into the complete prophecy, but some respected teachers of God's Word believe Ezekiel chapter 4 reveals the exact dates Israel would regain the land, and Jerusalem. If that be so, how can anyone believe the Jews aren't really the Jews? Would God allow impostor Jews to inhabit the parcel of ground He calls His own? Modern Israel isn't exactly spiritual, but to deny they are God's people isn't a particularly bright idea.

Again the word of the Lord of hosts came to me, saying, Thus saith the Lord of hosts; I was jealous for Zion with great jealousy, and I was jealous for her with great fury. Zechariah 8:1-2

They're God's people. Sure, they've got problems now — we all do — but those problems fail to negate the unconditional and irrevocable promises God made to them. It's grace, not works. They may not *deserve* what they've got (do any of us?), but they don't forfeit their inheritance. If you have children, do you disinherit them when they stumble? Of course not. Even the prodigal son never forfeited his sonship, even though his actions proved to be less than stellar.

Thus saith the Lord; I am returned unto Zion, and will dwell in the midst of Jerusalem; and Jerusalem shall be called a city of truth; and the mountain of the Lord of hosts the holy mountain. Zechariah 8:3

This obviously hasn't happened yet; it's still future, thus the Jews *must* still be God's people. This alone should settle the issue,

---

*   McGee (1982, page 951)

but a similar problem arises with Daniel's 70 week prophecy, where the text clearly involves the Jews only, and it's clear those events couldn't possibly have occurred yet (the end of sin, etc).

The only way out of the clear and obvious meaning of the text uses either allegories to avoid the obvious meaning, or state it doesn't apply for today. Once you travel down that road, what does any of the Bible (or anything else) really mean? Nothing means what it says, and text exists only as a paperclip waiting to be twisted into whatever shape desired.

We'll discuss exactly *how* that occurs later in the book when we discuss dialectic thought and its origins in post-modern philosophy. You'll need to understand some boring background, but once you do, you'll quickly spot many bizarre perversions of the text, including social justice, universal salvation, collective salvation, and others.

> *Thus saith the Lord of hosts; There shall yet old men and old women dwell in the streets of Jerusalem, and every man with his staff in his hand for very age. And the streets of the city shall be full of boys and girls playing in the streets thereof.*
> Zechariah 8:4–5

If you read the news at all, you know kids can't play in the street right now with bombings and other violent acts, so once again this remains yet future. Everyone desires peace in the Middle East, but it's quite unlikely until the Prince of Peace returns.

> *Thus saith the Lord of hosts; If it be marvelous in the eyes of the remnant of this people in these days, should it also be marvelous in mine eyes? saith the Lord of hosts. Thus saith the Lord of hosts; Behold, I will save my people from the east country, and from the west country; And I will bring them, and they shall dwell in the midst of Jerusalem; and they shall be my people, and I will be their God, in truth and in righteousness.*
> Zechariah 8:6–8

The regathering in the land in truth and righteousness. Once again, an event not happened yet. They may be back in the land, but Israel remains a basically secular country today. At some future point, they will turn their hearts back to God as they return to truth and righteousness.

> *Thus saith the Lord of hosts; Let your hands be strong, ye that hear in these days these words by the mouth of the prophets,*

> *which were in the day that the foundation of the house of the Lord of hosts was laid, that the temple might be built.*
>
> Zechariah 8:9

Be encouraged; Haggai and Zechariah say to Israel to get back in the game. It's the fourth quarter, you can't quit right now, the goal comes near. You must remember service for God is tough. It's not always fun, nor easy. Ignore what Paul called our "light afflictions" in 2 Corinthians 4:16–18, and look toward the certain future.

> *For before these days there was no hire for man, nor any hire for beast; neither was there any peace to him that went out or came in because of the affliction; for I set all men every one against his neighbor. But now I will not be unto the residue of this people as in the former days, saith the Lord of hosts.*
>
> Zechariah 8:10-11

Look to the future instead of current situations. It's not always going to be this way.

> *For the seed shall be prosperous; the vine shall give her fruit, and the ground shall give her increase, and the heavens shall give their dew; and I will cause the remnant of this people to possess all these things. And it shall come to pass, that as ye were a curse among the heathen, O house of Judah, and house of Israel; so will I save you, and ye shall be a blessing; fear not, but let your hands be strong.*
>
> Zechariah 8:12-13

The Jews are blamed for everything. Someone starts a war and Israel gets blamed for it, even if they had nothing to do with it. Right now many nations treat Israel as a curse, if only they would go away or give in we could have world peace. That's not true, of course, but it does seem to be the attitude of many people. God says a time will come when that deception no longer applies, and Israel will be a blessing once again.

> *For thus saith the Lord of hosts; As I thought to punish you, when your fathers provoked me to wrath, saith the Lord of hosts, and I repented not, So again have I thought in these days to do good unto Jerusalem and to the house of Judah; fear ye not.*
>
> Zechariah 8:14-15

ZECHARIAH

All through the Old Testament Israel abandons God and gets punished for it. Like any Father, the Lord corrects Israel when they disobey.

> *These are the things that ye shall do; Speak ye every man the truth to his neighbor; execute the judgment of truth and peace in your gates; And let none of you imagine evil in your hearts against his neighbor; and love no false oath; for all these are things that I hate, saith the Lord.* Zechariah 8:16–17

A reminder of the ten commandments. Thou shalt not kill. Thou shalt not commit adultery. Thou shalt not steal. Thou shalt not bear false witness against thy neighbor. Thou shalt not covet thy neighbor's house, thou shalt not covet thy neighbor's wife, nor his manservant, nor his maidservant, nor his ox, nor his donkey, nor any thing that is thy neighbor's (Exodus 20:13–17).

> *And the word of the Lord of hosts came unto me, saying, Thus saith the Lord of hosts; The fast of the fourth month, and the fast of the fifth, and the fast of the seventh, and the fast of the tenth, shall be to the house of Judah joy and gladness, and cheerful feasts; therefore love the truth and peace.* Zechariah 8:18–19

God changes fasts to feasts, desert to oasis, sadness to joy, and so on.

> *Thus saith the Lord of hosts; It shall yet come to pass, that there shall come people, and the inhabitants of many cities; And the inhabitants of one city shall go to another, saying, Let us go speedily to pray before the Lord, and to seek the Lord of hosts; I will go also.* Zechariah 8:20–21

If anything hasn't yet convinced you this is yet future, walk downtown in any medium city and see how many people grab you saying let's go quickly to pray. It won't happen. But it shall come to pass in one day that *will* be a common occurrence.

> *Yea, many people and strong nations shall come to seek the Lord of hosts in Jerusalem, and to pray before the Lord. Thus saith the Lord of hosts; In those days it shall come to pass, that ten men shall take hold out of all languages of the nations, even shall take hold of the skirt of him that is a Jew, saying, We will go with you; for we have heard that God is with you.* Zechariah 8:22–23

Jerusalem shall be the center of the world, as it's a small tract of land God Himself maintains keen interest in. At this (obviously still future) point, people will attach themselves to the Jews, as they'll see the true and living God dwells with the Jewish people. That's not exactly the view of people today, so once again we see what Zechariah says concerns future events.

CHAPTER XIV

Operational Pause

WE'RE GOING TO TAKE AN OPERATIONAL PAUSE TO see how we got here. While verse by verse teaching provides the best *overall* knowledge of the Bible, sometimes we lose the forest for the trees in detailed studies of specific areas, so we're going to take a step back and see where we came from. Recall the Jews lived in bondage, but Cyrus releases the Jews to return and build their temple. Only about 50,000 *did* return (Ezra 2:64–65), with the remainder preferring to live in bondage.

Those who returned began to rebuild the temple, but quit after coming under attack and the discouragement that followed. That's when God sends Zechariah and Haggai, encouraging the people for their task. After thousands of years, how can we find equal encouragement in our trials? Or is the book only good for historical analysis? The theme for Zechariah we've discussed since the beginning — *get back in the game*. Too many Christians sit on the sidelines either from laziness or from discouragement; if you're in the game you're going to take hits. Count on it.

That's all academic discussion ... what about where the rubber meets the road? What about the 3 AM call? What then? Ever feel like the Lord abandoned you? How can we today apply the practical application of Zechariah? You know, when you *really* need it? We look for answers or reason. Solomon tried and never found the answer he desperately sought, only concluding all is vanity.

Motorcycle riders have a saying only two types of riders exist — those that crashed, and those that are going to. In a similar vein, as a Christian you're either facing a trial, or you will soon be. Unfortunately, contrary to popular thought you will not rise to the occasion, you'll sink to the level of your training; Christians fail when they look in their toolbox and discover nothing there but empty space.

Acknowledge Reality

Let's take a trip in Mr. Peabody's wayback machine, back to the Jews building the wall in Nehemiah four. As Solomon discovered, there's nothing new under the sun, the same old problems the Jews faced we'll face today.

> *But it came to pass, that when Sanballat heard that we were building the wall, he was angry, and felt great indignation, and mocked the Jews. And he spoke before his brethren and the army of Samaria, and said, What are these feeble Jews doing? Will they fortify themselves? Will they sacrifice? Will they finish in a day?* Nehemiah 4:1–2a

It's everyone against them, as they're mocked for even *trying*. How many times have you been mocked for doing the Lord's work? It's not anything new, those mockings have occurred for thousands of years.

If you're a football fan, perhaps you've heard of Tim Tebow. If so, you've likely seen him pray during or after games, and of course that's just something that can't exist without mocking. It's called "tebowing," that is to take a knee and pray, even if everyone around you does something different. Why the disdain for Tim Tebow? Why mock him so much?

He's not the originator of the idea anyway. It began with a few Jewish guys named Hananiah, Mishael, and Azariah. Perhaps you've heard the story in Daniel 3. Remember when the command came to bow down and worship the idol? They refused to follow the herd and do what everyone else did, and I suspect (even though it's not mentioned) they were praying quite a bit.

Mocking God's people isn't new, and it won't go away. If you're working on God's assignments, you can *guarantee* you'll be mocked. I'm sure Noah endured the same thing while building the ark; in the end he was proven correct. As John Loeffler says, "your failure to be informed does not make me a wacko."

> *Now Tobiah the Ammonite was by him, and he said, Even that which they build, if a fox go up, he shall even break down their stone wall.* Nehemiah 4:3

Whatever they're doing isn't worth it, and will fall as a bunch of groups conspire to fight against it. What did the Jews do? Cower in fear? Quit? Nope, they stayed in the game. Don't give in to the mocking. Sure it will come, but you should ignore it and stay the course.

> *Nevertheless we made our prayer unto our God, and set a watch against them day and night, because of them.*
> Nehemiah 4:9

A Time to Fight, a Time to Blow the Trumpet

You must acquire a true perception of reality. The Jews were prepared, but refused to quit.

> *For the builders, every one had his sword girded by his side, and so builded. And he that sounded the trumpet was by me.*
> Nehemiah 4:18

The individuals worked, but prepared for an attack, *while they did the work*. It's foolish to fail in your preparations when you know the enemy lies in wait for the most opportune moment to strike. What was the trumpet for?

> *And I said unto the nobles, and to the rulers, and to the rest of the people, The work is great and large, and we are separated upon the wall, one far from another. In what place therefore ye hear the sound of the trumpet, resort ye there unto us. Our God shall fight for us.*
> Nehemiah 4:19-20

One person blows the trumpet for reinforcements; even though God fights for us, we need reinforcements. Times exist you need help, so blow the trumpet and let people rally around. Foolish is the person adopting a go-it-alone mentality — an idea not promoted in the Bible. When you're under attack, blow the trumpet.

As always, two extremes exist, both prove wrong. The first comes from people constantly whining about everything instead of getting off their couch and trying to handle the situation themselves. Those people need to learn to provide for themselves.

The second problem comes from the plastic Christian smile as people refuse to admit they're hurting and in a bad situation. Obviously, if every time someone asks how you're doing you unload, you'll become like the previous person. However, if you're good at plastering a fake smile and denying reality, that's no good either.

Don't become a Tony the Tiger Christian, where everything is grrrrreat! The church should be a friendly place where people can assist one another through life's trials. If you're not availing yourself of the assistance, you're not functioning as the church should. Blow the trumpet as Nehemiah did — let's not play church and be Tony the Tiger Christians.

Why Dost Thou Doubt?

Don't think you're all alone, or that someone else should do the work. Either error creates problems. You need a reasonable, balanced approach; you should never be afraid to ask for help, but you also should never dump on people and expect them to constantly bail you out.

Peter might be my favorite guy — we can relate to him. The only time he opened his mouth was to change feet — socially challenged you might say. In Matthew 14, after the feeding of the 5,000 we have an interesting event providing insight.

> *And straightway Jesus constrained his disciples to get into a boat, and to go before him unto the other side, while he sent the multitudes away. And when he had sent the multitudes away, he went up into a mountain privately to pray; and when the evening was come, he was there alone. But the boat was now in the midst of the sea, tossed with waves; for the wind was contrary.* Matthew 14:22-24

Feel like that? You told me to do this, Lord, and now it's a mess, with everything against me. Like the Jews, Zechariah speaks to us with encouragement of the future.

> *And in the fourth watch of the night Jesus went unto them, walking on the sea. And when the disciples saw him walking on the sea, they were troubled, saying, It is a ghost; and they cried out for fear.* Matthew 14:25-26

Legend has it they believed right before you died you'd see ghosts on the water, so these professional fishermen didn't have much optimism for the remainder of their journey.

> *But straightway Jesus spoke unto them, saying, Be of good cheer; it is I; be not afraid.* Matthew 14:27

That message doesn't change circumstances much. They're still in trouble, still afraid, still wondering if they'll make it across. Jesus appears, and says don't worry about it. Notice He never says you won't go through storms, only He'll be with you always. The question is do you believe it? Imagine some of the possible trials you could be going through right now.

1. "I've been betrayed."
2. "I'm hated for no reason."
3. "I'm innocent."

Each of those Jesus Himself understands. Your situation isn't something ever experienced before. We have a God who understands your particular situation, and still says to you be of good cheer, don't be afraid. Will you listen, or not?

And Peter answered him and said, Lord, if it be thou, bid me come unto thee on the water. And he said, Come. And when Peter was come down out of the boat, he walked on the water, to go to Jesus. Matthew 14:28–29

Peter did what he usually did — bold action. But then he also did what he usually did, he ran into problems.

But when he saw the wind boisterous, he was afraid; and beginning to sink, he cried, saying, Lord, save me.
Matthew 14:30

Our cry as well, Lord save me! Forgotten in all the panic remains the Lord's simple truth: didn't I say to go to the other side?

And immediately Jesus stretched forth his hand, and caught him, and said unto him, O thou of little faith, why didst thou doubt? And when they were come into the boat, the wind ceased. Matthew 14:31–32

When trials come up you must ask — faith or foam? It's your choice. That's where we arrive at ... faith or foam, because no other option exists. You can persevere and continue, or quit in despair and frustration. But when you take your eyes off Jesus, you'll meet the foam.

Clay Without Fire is Useless

When you have no hope of supporting yourself standing on water, it's faith or foam. Peter wasn't the first person to face the choice, nor the last. You can't "sort of" follow Jesus — you're either in or out. If you're in, understand your relationship with the Lord, as Jeremiah 18 relates with the potter and clay.

> *The word which came to Jeremiah from the Lord, saying, Arise, and go down to the potter's house, and there I will cause thee to hear my words. Then I went down to the potter's house, and, behold, he wrought a work on the wheels. And the vessel that he made of clay was marred in the hand of the potter; so he made it again another vessel, as seemed good to the potter to make it.*
>
> *Then the word of the Lord came to me, saying, O house of Israel, cannot I do with you as this potter? saith the Lord. Behold, as the clay is in the potter's hand, so are ye in mine hand, O house of Israel.* Jeremiah 18:1–6

When the maker molds the clay, it's still clay. Sure it may look a bit different (like a pot instead of a lump), but it's still clay. After forming the clay the potter places it in the fire; when the clay comes out of the fire it looks the same, but isn't; the fire changes the clay, and *those changes are irreversible.*

If you create a clay pot and don't fire it, what happens when you put water in it? It reverts back to clay (in other words, it's useless). Fire changes the clay and *makes the vessel useful.* I'm sure if you asked the pot (and the clay could talk) it wouldn't like the fire. In fact, it would want to avoid it. In the middle of a hot trial we lose focus of the future, but the Lord doesn't because He already knows the next principle.

You are not Alone

A story exists (I don't remember where it came from, or even if it's true) about our pilots in WWII going over to fight for the first time alongside British pilots, who of course had been fighting for quite some time. When one pilot nervously wondered what happens if they spotted a huge gaggle of Germans the seasoned veteran replied "Rejoice, lad, that's why you're here."

The same idea applies to the Christian — you're a soldier with armor provided by the creator of the universe. When opposition

ZECHARIAH

arises in your service to God, don't be surprised. All that's great, you say, but you don't know what I'm going through, it's tough. Perhaps not, but Paul sure did.

> *For we would not, brethren, have you ignorant of our trouble which came to us in Asia, that we were pressed out of measure, above strength, insomuch that we despaired even of life. But we had the sentence of death in ourselves, that we should not trust in ourselves, but in God which raiseth the dead.*
>
> 2 Corinthians 1:8–9

Paul, despaired even of life? I think that covers quite a bit, as above strength implies more than he could bear. Have you ever felt like that? Overwhelmed? Hopeless? Most of us have sometime. Satan wants you to believe nobody understands your situation so you'll be isolated. Don't buy it. Do what Nehemiah did — blow the trumpet! Rally the troops because you're not alone, no matter what it feels like. Recall Paul a little later in Corinthians:

> *We are troubled on every side, yet not distressed; we are perplexed, but not in despair*
>
> 2 Corinthians 4:8

Avail Yourself of Help

We continually discuss the armor of God, but in all the discussion one crucial element is almost always missed — soldiers don't go to battle by themselves. Why do Christians frequently attempt such a foolish move as engaging in battle without backup? The go-it-alone mentality is nothing more than tactics from the enemy. You've got to blow the trumpet.

Good and bad happens to everyone in life, that's just reality. If you've been through a specific tough situation, you're uniquely qualified to assist others to also make it through. On the flip side, if you're in a tough trial now, it's likely someone else has crawled over the same ground before as well.

If you're not using your fellow soldiers, you're not being all you can be. Another reason not to be a Tony the Tiger Christian, a familiar situation in churches as everyone plasters on the phony Christian smile proclaiming it's grrrrreat, when it's not.

Christianity isn't Sunday Only

> *But now thus saith the Lord that created thee, O Jacob, and he that formed thee, O Israel, Fear not; for I have redeemed*

> *thee, I have called thee by thy name; thou art mine. When thou passest through the waters, I will be with thee; and through the rivers, they shall not overflow thee; when thou walkest through the fire, thou shalt not be burned; neither shall the flame kindle upon thee.*
>
> Isaiah 43:1-2

When you go through the fire, in other words it's guaranteed. Jesus Himself proclaimed you *will* have tribulation — don't be surprised when it comes. Recall Hananiah, Mishael, and Azariah of Daniel 3 as they came through the fire unscathed ("whose bodies the fire had no power, nor was an hair of their head singed, neither were their coats changed, nor the smell of fire had passed on them").

When their 3 AM call came, they were ready. But they had no guarantee of what would happen. God's promise to be with you is not a promise of a painless life, or the situation will turn out how *you* want. Those three Hebrews had no idea how the situation would turn out as they stood before the king. Neither do you in your fiery trials. Those Hebrews clung to one thing: God will either deliver you from the trial or through the trial.

That doesn't mean life will be easy, wealthy, fun, or even as long as you wish. Each person has an amount of time allocated to them, and (as Daniel would say) when your number's up, it's up. That time could come today, tomorrow, or 50 years from now, but it can't be changed, so why worry about it? You can't affect it anyway.

We also must check our attitude towards God. We pray and God answers — the test is negative, or benign — Oh, we say, God is good! Yet does God's nature change if the test is positive? Or the cancer is inoperable? Does our attitude change a bit? It sure does, but wait a minute — did God's nature change ... or only our attitude? God is good, God is just, God is love — no matter what happens.

You *will* have 3 AM moments, are you prepared? Is it still raining? Do you have your sword ready at your side? Never forget Job chapter 2 verse 10 — "Shall we indeed accept good from God, and shall we not accept adversity?" Job might just have been the first beach-dude weight-lifter coining the phrase "no pain, no gain," or as we now understand: *adversity is the fire that makes clay useful*, transforming it from a chuck of mud into a tool to be used.

Romans 8:28 Still Exists

If you don't have a tab in Romans, you should.

And we know that all things work together for good to them that love God, to them who are the called according to His purpose.
Romans 8:28

It does *not* say you'll understand. It does mean when Jesus says "let's go to the other side of the lake" you'll make it, but that does not mean it's a cruise (we're no different from Israel in Zechariah's time). They started to follow God, build the temple, but got stuck, and quit. Zechariah and Haggai appear, and Zechariah shows the end — sure, you may be in tough times now, but the light at the end of the tunnel is *not* an oncoming freight train (apologies to Wile E. Coyote who always found the opposite).

The end is sure. The message of Zechariah/Haggai remains simple: Get Back in the Game!

Content. That's the word. A state of heart in which you would be at peace if God gave you nothing more than he already has. Test yourself with this question: What if God's only gift to you were his grace to save you. Would you be content? You beg him to save the life of your child. You plead with him to keep your business afloat. You implore him to remove the cancer from your body. What if his answer is, "My grace is enough." Would you be content?*

If you recall the old movie "Wall Street" Hal Holbrook's character uttered a strange phrase — "A man looks in the abyss, and sees nothing staring back at him but empty space. At that moment, a man finds his character, and that is what keeps him out of the abyss."

For Christians, you don't find your character, but a new reliance and trust in the Lord, and that keeps you out of the abyss. It's time to get in the game — service for God is tough.

---

*   Lucado (2005, page 131)

CHAPTER XIV. OPERATIONAL PAUSE

CHAPTER XV

Zechariah: First Coming of Christ

ZECHARIAH AND HAGGAI APPEAR ON THE SCENE to encourage the people to build the temple, in other words to get back in the game. They respond, complete the temple, and by the time we find ourselves at chapter 9 we've come to the dreaded question — so what? We've returned from slavery, begun the work, got discouraged, then got back in the game. Now what? Where do we go from here?

First, focus on the return of Christ for the remainder of the book. When Zechariah penned his book, the remainder of the book (chapters 9–14) were yet future. From our perspective, chapters 9–11 detail the first coming of Christ (historical), while chapters 12–14 detail the future second coming of Christ.

Second, the remarkable discovery awaiting you after you discover Christianity isn't a Sunday and Wednesday idea (not the fire extinguisher on the wall, "in case of crisis break glass") — it's how you live your daily life. It involves *every* part of your life; no separate God box exists. To paraphrase Zechariah — not by slogan, nor by feelings, but by my spirit, saith the Lord.

Sure, you're saved, but does it make an impact? Can you sit in church and listen for years, and fail to put into practice what you know to be true? Of course. Nobody forces you to do anything — you're a free person to do as you wish. That doesn't mean it's a good idea, however.

For the Jews, they've accomplished what they needed to, so now look to the relationship, and their ultimate hope — the Messiah. In chapter 9, verses 1–8 detail Alexander's conquest of the world, with the curious note Jerusalem isn't destroyed. As we saw with Daniel, liberal critics attempt to "late date" Zechariah as they do with Daniel simply because they don't like the idea of a God providing details of future events (like Daniel, Zechariah was part of the Septuagint as historical record, so they've got a problem).

> *The burden of the word of the Lord in the land of Hadrach, and Damascus shall be the rest thereof, when the eyes of man, as of all the tribes of Israel, shall be toward the Lord.* Zechariah 9:1

All eyes turn toward the Lord — it's a crisis! It's common to ignore the Lord except in times of crisis, and then we sure do remember Him, don't we? Yet the Lord has interest in a relationship, and perhaps sometimes just might allow trials so we don't forget Him.

> *And Hamath also shall border thereby; Tyrus, and Zidon, though it be very wise. And Tyrus did build herself a strong hold, and heaped up silver as the dust, and fine gold as the mire of the streets. Behold, the Lord will cast her out, and he will smite her power in the sea; and she shall be devoured with fire.* Zechariah 9:2-4

We'll skip much of the history of Tyre (some of which Ezekiel provides in chapter 26), as Alexander the Great & Nebuchadnezzar both tried to take the city; Nebuchadnezzar couldn't after years of siege; Alexander was a bit more creative and managed to take the city in less than a year.

> *Ashkelon shall see it, and fear; Gaza also shall see it, and be very sorrowful, and Ekron; for her expectation shall be ashamed; and the king shall perish from Gaza, and Ashkelon shall not be inhabited. And a bastard shall dwell in Ashdod, and I will cut off the pride of the Philistines. And I will take away his blood out of his mouth, and his abominations from between his teeth; but he that remaineth, even he, shall be for our God, and he shall be as a governor in Judah, and Ekron as a Jebusite.* Zechariah 9:5-7

Alexander travels down to Israel. Since we look at it today as historical (though prophecy at Zechariah's time), we'll skip a detailed analysis. The KJV uses "bastard"; one of those words not a lot of people know the true definition of anymore (other translations call it a mixed race, which is a bit more modern). They lost their identity, and after Alexander was done, it was more of a mixed tribe than an identifiable group.

ZECHARIAH

> *And I will encamp about mine house because of the army, because of him that passeth by, and because of him that returneth; and no oppressor shall pass through them any more; for now have I seen with mine eyes.* Zechariah 9:8

Alexander conquerors the known world, now arriving at Jerusalem. As recorded in Josephus Book XI, Chapter VII, Section 5, the priests go out to meet him, and present him the prophecy of Daniel; it impresses Alexander so much he spares the city. Alexander conquers with flair, calling attention to himself. Now compare the history to the future coming of the Messiah.

> *Rejoice greatly, O daughter of Zion; shout, O daughter of Jerusalem; behold, thy King cometh unto thee; he is just, and having salvation; lowly, and riding upon a donkey, and upon a colt the foal of a donkey.* Zechariah 9:9

In contrast to the human conquerors, He is just and humble, providing victory. This verse in Zechariah could be one of the most memorable, as it looks forward to what we call Palm Sunday. Jesus held them accountable to understand the prophecy, as in Luke 19 Jesus weeps over the city as the exact day predicted by Daniel in the famous 70 week prophecy.

> *And I will cut off the chariot from Ephraim, and the horse from Jerusalem, and the battle bow shall be cut off; and he shall speak peace unto the nations; and his dominion shall be from sea even to sea, and from the river even to the ends of the earth.* Zechariah 9:10

This verse implies a gap between verse 9 and 10. Why? Common sense. Verse 9 clearly describes the first coming of Christ, while in verse 10 peace comes to Israel — something that won't happen until the return of Christ. Today if Israel lays down their weapons they cease to exist, thus verse 10 remains yet future.

> *As for thee also, by the blood of thy covenant I have sent forth thy prisoners out of the pit wherein is no water. Turn you to the strong hold, ye prisoners of hope; even today do I declare that I will render double unto thee;* Zechariah 9:11-12

God made many covenants with man — beginning with Adam, then Abraham, Moses, and so on. He holds to those promises and won't break them, so when you see the Word of the Lord you can be confident, as God is a God of consistency. The only reason science and other disciplines work comes from God's creation being orderly and following consistent rules.

It's interesting even atheists and scientists follow the consistency of God without admitting it. The only way we can understand *anything* about the universe is because God created it ordered and following specific rules, rules waiting to be discovered.

> *When I have bent Judah for me, filled the bow with Ephraim, and raised up thy sons, O Zion, against thy sons, O Greece, and made thee as the sword of a mighty man. And the Lord shall be seen over them, and his arrow shall go forth as the lightning; and the Lord God shall blow the trumpet, and shall go with whirlwinds of the south. The Lord of hosts shall defend them; and they shall devour, and subdue the sling stones; and they shall drink, and make a noise as through wine; and they shall be filled like bowls, and as the corners of the altar. And the Lord their God shall save them in that day as the flock of his people; for they shall be as the stones of a crown, lifted up as an ensign upon his land.* Zechariah 9:13–16

The defeat of Greece, a matter of historical fact.

> *For how great is his goodness, and how great is his beauty! Grain shall make the young men cheerful, and new wine the maids.* Zechariah 9:17

In contrast with Alexander, the Lord delivers and provides for His people. You might believe in your present situation God fails to provide (at least the way you want), but nevertheless behind the scenes you can remain confident in the end everything works out (Romans 8:28 still exists ... I checked).

> *Ask ye of the Lord rain in the time of the latter rain; so the Lord shall make bright clouds, and give them showers of rain, to every one grass in the field.* Zechariah 10:1

This verse actually belongs in chapter 9, as it concludes the thought of the deliverance of Israel. Don't make the mistake chapter and verse breaks in the Bible are of divine origin. They exist only as a quick way to find specific sections, and sometimes breaks appear in less than desirable places.

Jon Courson notes when the Jews were dispersed in 70 AD and the Turks gained control of the land, they taxed people by how many trees existed on their land. You can imagine what came next, as a desire to lower tax bills remains universal throughout the world. It doesn't take long to figure out how to trim the tax bill, so the land became deforested, which changed the climate in that area quite a bit.

Zechariah reminds us to ask of the Lord; Paul says we come boldly to the throne of grace, and James says you have not because you ask not, or because you ask for your own pleasures (like a Lexus). Many people fear coming to God with "small" requests thinking God only handles the big problems. Not so.

God is interested in fellowship, and wants to hear from you in all things. Yes, that means even the little things. Don't forget God is not your genie, so if you're praying for a pony, don't be surprised when you open your eyes and find nothing magically appeared. Sure, you know that already, but how often do you think it without acknowledging it?

> *For the idols have spoken vanity, and the diviners have seen a lie, and have told false dreams; they comfort in vain; therefore they went their way as a flock, they were troubled, because there was no shepherd.* Zechariah 10:2

Divination attempts to see the future. Like many things in the Bible, we think we're past these primitive problems, yet the desire to see the future remains a strong temptation with man. How many people read their horoscope? Check out the predictions for the new year in the supermarket tabloids?

Nothing changes. From reading tea leaves and palms, to reading the liver as the Babylonians (Ezekiel 21:21), the methods change, but mans' desire to know what the future holds remains a strong draw, just as it did thousands of years ago.

Yet God forbids it; recall Saul and the witch of Endor in 1 Samuel 28. First, Saul's desire to communicate with people already dead (another bad idea persisting for thousands of years), but also notice the medium's shock when Samuel really *does* appear — an admission these séances and other occult practices turn out to be fake (you might remember Houdini sought for years to communicate with the dead, yet found all attempts to be phony).

Many false "prophets" simply tell you what you want to hear ("comfort in vain" as Zechariah says). It's *easy* to say you'll be rich, have a Lexus and so on. Those speaking false ideas in God's name can be popular, write books, have influence with politicians, and more. But they're still false prophets speaking lies.

Look up 1 Kings 22 for an example, and note that listening to those people doesn't end well. God's word may not always be popular, but it *will* be true (see also Ezekiel 13:1–8). If you obtain meaning from popular (but false) prophets, you'll be troubled because you've abandoned the shepherd.

Why do we do it? Why is the National Enquirer so popular, with horoscopes and such? We must turn back to one of my favorite stories — the disciples on the lake in Mark 4:35–40. What did they lack? They lacked faith in God's plan. Sure, they knew who Jesus was, they knew He could help — what they forgot was Jesus' earlier words *let's go to the other side.*

We frequently lack the same faith in God's Word, that's why we look for the future, ultimately it's a lack of faith in God's plan — did God *really* say that? Did He mean it? Let me have a peek into the future, and then I'll have faith. But it doesn't work that way. Faith comes first, and then you'll discover you don't need your horoscope anymore.

> *For I know the thoughts that I think toward you, saith the Lord, thoughts of peace, and not of evil, to give you an expected end.*
> Jeremiah 29:11

An expected end? Isn't that what Jesus gave the disciples? They didn't accept it, and many times we don't either, thus the desire for fortune telling continues to this day. Of course, God's assurance of an expected end doesn't mean to be unprepared for possibilities, or do something stupid to tempt God, but don't worry about the future or attempt to divine it. That's a form of idolatry. What's an idol? Anything taking the place of God, in this case, knowledge of future events.

> *Mine anger was kindled against the shepherds, and I punished the goats; for the Lord of hosts hath visited his flock the house of Judah, and hath made them as his majestic horse in the battle.*
> Zechariah 10:3

Those false shepherds lead astray the flock. Perhaps nothing is more serious than a false teacher leading astray the people of God. Remember those false teachers can have best-seller books, influence with politicians and others, be famous, rich, and popular ... but they're still false teachers.

The Bible forms ideology, not ideology forming the Bible (their preferred method for heretical ideas comes from using postmodern philosophy, an idea we'll cover later). In that perverted vein, some redefine clear Biblical ideas, and then try to con you into buying their trash. Even if they sound Christian and use the right terms, you must recognize under their thin candy shell of Christianity lays a toxic goo of heresy.

Most people understand heretics exist, but they're used to seeing them wild-eyed on TV and spouting crazy ideas. As we discussed way back in the introduction, people might be shocked to find heretics can inhabit popular pulpits and peddle best selling books. Never forget heresy does not define itself by popularity or lack of popularity, but how someone views the Word of God. Do they twist it, and tell you their ideas may not exactly be in the Bible, but you should accept them anyway?

> *But there were false prophets also among the people, even as there shall be false teachers among you, who secretly shall bring in damnable heresies, even denying the Lord that bought them, and bring upon themselves swift destruction. And many shall follow their pernicious ways; by reason of whom the way of truth shall be evil spoken of.* 2 Peter 2:1-2

There *will* be false teachers in the church, just as there were in Israel. We could list some popular fads floating around (collective salvation, replacement theology, social justice, red letter Christianity, emergent church, and so on), but notice many aren't new; deception has existed for centuries; even CS Lewis warned about (what today is) a popular fad.

> *On the other hand we do want, and want very much, to make men treat Christianity as a means; preferably, of course, as a means to their own advancement, but, failing that, as a means to anything—even to social justice. The thing to do is get a man at first to value social justice as a thing which the Enemy demands, and work him on to the stage at which he values Christianity because it may produce social justice.*
>
> *... I have found a passage in a Christian writer where he recommends his own version of Christianity on the ground that "only such a faith can outlast the death of old cultures and new civilizations." You see the little rift? "Believe this, not because it is true, but for some other reason." That's the game.**

---
*   Lewis (1990, page 119-120)

It's always interesting when people notice the lies, but can't figure out why. If you can't figure out why, it means you're susceptible to falling for deception. What's the antidote for false teaching? Knowing the truth so you can spot the phony. Many false ideas wrap themselves in Christian sounding terms so people fall for them. At 3 AM when the phone rings you've got what you've got — it's too late to figure out what you believe and why. As a soldier of God, you need to be prepared *before* the battle you know will soon arrive.

> *Out of him came forth the corner, out of him the nail, out of him the battle bow, out of him every oppressor together.*
> Zechariah 10:4

Out of whom? Judah. The one who is to come. The Messiah. He's the cornerstone. Note immediately after the warning about occult and false teachers, the true Messiah is presented. Jesus is the cornerstone, the foundation of all. You can either accept or reject it as you wish, but your failure to accept the truth does not cause truth to become untruth.

A nail is what you hang something on. Your life, your total existence should hang on Him. Not divination or occult to find the future, but total trust in Him.

> *And they shall be as mighty men, which tread down their enemies in the mire of the streets in the battle; and they shall fight, because the Lord is with them, and the riders on horses shall be confounded. And I will strengthen the house of Judah, and I will save the house of Joseph, and I will bring them again to place them; for I have mercy upon them, and they shall be as though I had not cast them off; for I am the Lord their God, and will hear them. And they of Ephraim shall be like a mighty man, and their heart shall rejoice as through wine; yea, their children shall see it, and be glad; their heart shall rejoice in the Lord.*
> Zechariah 10:5–7

It doesn't matter the odds, God's plan can't be thwarted. You may not see what's going on, but that doesn't mean God's plan isn't at work. Remember 2 Kings 6 with Elisha and the servant as the Syrian army surrounds them. The servant wakes up in a panic, while Elisha sleeps comfortably. What's the difference? The servant wasn't thinking fourth dimensionally. Elisha understood the real reality, while the servant accepted only what he could see, continually pestering Elisha about what he perceived to be a big problem.

Elisha discovers he won't sleep until he solves the servant's little problem, so he prays for God to open his servant's eyes to see. Once he did, the servant feels better. But wait, did the servant's window into alternate dimensions suddenly change the situation? Of course not. What it did do is change his heart.

> *I will whistle for them, and gather them; for I have redeemed them, and they shall increase as they have increased.*
> Zechariah 10:8

Some commentators believe as many as 12 million Jews lived in the land before the Romans destroyed the city in 70 AD. Today it's about 7.5 million. It may not be flattering, but it's like you whistling for your dog. Here boy, come here! Back in the land again. It's amazing how much theology you can learn from your dog.

> *And I will sow them among the peoples; and they shall remember me in far countries; and they shall live with their children, and turn again.*
> Zechariah 10:9

They will turn back to God. One purpose of the tribulation is to wake up the nation of Israel. Mixing up the church and the Jews causes all sorts of trouble; they're distinct and separate.

> *I will bring them again also out of the land of Egypt, and gather them out of Assyria; and I will bring them into the land of Gilead and Lebanon; and place shall not be found for them. And he shall pass through the sea with affliction, and shall smite the waves in the sea, and all the deeps of the river shall dry up; and the pride of Assyria shall be brought down, and the scepter of Egypt shall depart away.*
> Zechariah 10:10–11

Guess who wins in the end? You may be discouraged about seeing evil appear to win, but that's not a permanent situation. They're not getting by with it, and God does notice.

The promises to Abraham and the Jews regarding the land are unconditional and irrevocable. They still have a destiny to be fulfilled in the land. We should recall the words "I will bless them that bless thee, and curse them that curse thee" as we mess around with Middle East policy.

> *And I will strengthen them in the Lord; and they shall walk up and down in his name, saith the Lord.* Zechariah 10:12

It's a bit clearer in the New Living Translation: "I will make my people strong in my power, and they will go wherever they wish by my authority. I, the Lord, have spoken." As a famous Charlton Heston movie about the Ten Commandments said "so it is written, so it shall be."

> *Open thy doors, O Lebanon, that the fire may devour thy cedars. Wail, fir tree; for the cedar is fallen; because the mighty are spoiled; wail, O ye oaks of Bashan; for the forest of the vintage is come down. There is a voice of the wailing of the shepherds; for their glory is spoiled; a voice of the roaring of young lions; for the pride of Jordan is spoiled.* Zechariah 11:1-3

The shepherds predict peace and prosperity, but turn out to be false. False shepherds (in our time we call them pastors) tell people what they want to hear, but then the people are slaughtered when the truth turns out to be different. Frankly I'm tired of watching that happen; it's time for all of us to get back in the game, repel false prophets, and proclaim truth; you'll encounter two types of people in your mission.

The first, those honestly desiring to understand God and meet Him, but have been victims of incorrect teaching (or no teaching at all), and thus are living in The Matrix. For those people, education supplies the answer. You don't need to be hostile or combative (not a good idea anyway) as these people will usually grasp at truth as soon as you present it, since they're open minded and actively searching.

The second group is much harder. They're the group that wants to deceive you. They know they're using alternate definitions of the gospel, for example, but for their own political, social, or theological reasons they refuse to accept truth, and actively promote their deceptions to others. For people in this group, they're definitely aware they're living in The Matrix of deception.

You can't do much for that group. They already know they're deceived, they're promoting deception, and they're against the Bible ... but they don't care. All you can do is remind them of their position, and hope someday they'll desire to change. This group Jude warns against in his letter, sometimes referred to as the acts of the apostates. Unfortunately, this chapter isn't as much fun as the rest of the book, but deception and false hope by phony prophets remains as real today as in the days of Jeremiah.

Then the Lord said unto me, The prophets prophesy lies in my name. I sent them not, neither have I commanded them, neither spoke unto them; they prophesy unto you a false vision and divination, and a thing of nought, and the deceit of their heart.

Therefore thus saith the Lord concerning the prophets that prophesy in my name, and I sent them not, yet they say, Sword and famine shall not be in this land; By sword and famine shall those prophets be consumed. Jeremiah 14:14-15

It's no mystery developing a large church, simply tell people what they want to hear and don't mention sin (at least don't use God's rules), repentance, hell, or responsibility. Tell them good works are acceptable to God, and much of the Bible needs to be reinterpreted for today so many uncomfortable sections no longer apply to our lives. If you do that (and some do), you'll quickly have a rousing, large, popular — but dead — church.

Misrepresenting God is a big deal, as Moses found out. As he led the Jews out of Egypt you'll find two events that upon first glance appear to be the same event, as twice the people grumble about their lack of provision and water. Both times God gives Moses instructions involving a rock.

Unfortunately, the second time Moses didn't exactly follow directions, and while God still provides water for the people, He takes Moses aside later and informs him since he didn't exactly follow His instructions he can't enter the promised land.

That's not fair! Moses led the people out of Egypt and for years led them in the wilderness, and for one small mistake gets benched? God takes misrepresenting Him very seriously.

Liberal theology substitutes man's value-relativism for the solid rock of God's Word. They may *sound* Christian, may *act* Christian, all the while trying to deceive you. And why not? For Satan himself transforms to an angel of light. If someone comes up to you and says, "I'm here to deceive you and draw you away from God's Word" you'll immediately recoil.

But if they slither in under names like scholarship, good works, modernizing, and a whole host of other fully buzzword-compliant terms, you might not notice the poison they're trying to cram down your throat, poison you swallow at your peril. When some slimy heretic slithers up to you proclaiming ideas like the Bible needs to be changed to fit with modern society, always recall what Walter Martin said.

Whenever I hear people make statements I very much like to know what they mean by the words because if they can't define the words in context they don't mean anything.

You must force them to define their terms, and once you do you'll discover terms like Jesus, sin, God, resurrection, hell, and more have all been changed from what the Bible says about them. If they use the same words with different definitions, you're not talking about the same thing at all. Yet telling people what they want to hear gets a big following; Zechariah warns trouble will arrive.

> *Thus saith the Lord my God; Feed the flock of the slaughter; Whose possessors slay them, and hold themselves not guilty; and they that sell them say, Blessed be the Lord; for I am rich; and their own shepherds pity them not.* Zechariah 11:4-5

A Shepherd should protect the flock, not fleece them for profit. These false prophets make large sums of money, deceive the people, and hold themselves guiltless. Fortunately, God notices; any teacher of God's Word (honest or otherwise) will have a stricter judgment of God, as God takes His word seriously.

> *For I will no more pity the inhabitants of the land, saith the Lord, but, lo, I will deliver the men every one into his neighbor's hand, and into the hand of his king; and they shall smite the land, and out of their hand I will not deliver them.* Zechariah 11:6

In Genesis 15 God makes an unconditional promise to Abraham, while other promises had both conditional and unconditional areas. A heresy floats around saying God cast off the Jews and the church now lives in its place. Not so, but that error can stem from some of the *conditional* promises God made — if the Jews do this, God does that and so on. They're *accountable* to understand, as Jesus notes.

> *And when he was come near, he beheld the city, and wept over it, Saying, If thou hadst known, even thou, at least in this thy day, the things which belong unto thy peace! but now they are hid from thine eyes. For the days shall come upon thee, that thine enemies shall cast a trench about thee, and compass thee round, and keep thee in on every side, And shall lay thee even with the ground, and thy children within thee; and they shall not leave in thee one stone upon another; because thou knewest not the time of thy visitation.* Luke 19:41-44

Matthew 24:15 "When ye therefore shall see the abomination of desolation, spoken of by Daniel the prophet, stand in the holy place, (whoso readeth, let him understand)." Are you reading? Then you're called to understand Daniel's prophecy.

If you're familiar with the Bible and prophecy in general, you'll recognize those false shepherds creeping in that Jude warns about. If not, you'll fall for the deception. All of us *will* have that 3 AM moment, and when you do, you've got what you've got. If you're trained and well-equipped, you'll likely do well. If unprepared, well ... not so much. Do you want to be the pig, or Chuck Norris? We thought so. One difference between the pig and Chuck Norris remains simple — the pig sits around all day being a sloth, while Chuck Norris trains and prepares.

A myth exists when crisis arrives you'll rise to the occasion. But that's not true. You won't rise to the occasion you'll sink to the level of your training. The question is, what is the status of your training? Prepared you must be, or fail you will. In other words, it's time to dig in and be serious. Train like you'll fight, so you'll fight like you trained (by the way, if you're reading this you can't say you never heard the warning; Matthew just told you).

> *And I will feed the flock of slaughter, even you, O poor of the flock. And I took unto me two staves; the one I called Beauty, and the other I called Bands; and I fed the flock.* Zechariah 11:7

Beauty means grace or favor, it's the shepherds crook we've all seen. It's used to nudge the sheep (subtly or not so subtly) back in line. Bands means covenant or union, the shepherds stick or club used to ward off or defend against predators. Similar to the rod and staff of Psalm 23 — it's two-fold protection. First, to keep you on the correct path with correction, and second, to protect you from those who would tear you to pieces.

> *Three shepherds also I cut off in one month; and my soul loathed them, and their soul also abhorred me.* Zechariah 11:8

Many commentators take these three shepherds to be three groups Jesus squared off against.

- Pharisees — legalists.
- Sadducees — liberals (or progressives).
- Herodians — political action group.

These three groups still exist today.

> *Then said I, I will not feed you; that that dieth, let it die; and that that is to be cut off, let it be cut off; and let the rest eat every one the flesh of another.*
> Zechariah 11:9

The flock will be fed no longer. Why? They rejected the true shepherd, and the Lord doesn't force you into anything. The Jews said "we will not have this man rule over us," and that's exactly what they got.

Recall after leaving Egypt the same thing occurs. They cry out why did you bring us out here to die? They refused to enter the promised land, and so the Lord says you want to die in the wilderness, go right ahead.

Why does God allow evil in the world? If God is love, and He's all powerful, why doesn't He *do* something? One simple reason — He won't force Himself on anyone; you can choose to follow God or not. Since God doesn't force Himself on you, you're free to accept or reject Him as you wish. But you can't choose the results of those choices, and if you choose poorly...

> *And I took my staff, even Beauty, and cut it asunder, that I might break my covenant which I had made with all the people. And it was broken in that day; and so the poor of the flock that waited upon me knew that it was the word of the Lord.*
> Zechariah 11:10-11

A *conditional* covenant. The people didn't do what they were supposed to, so the promise becomes void. Don't confuse conditional promises of God with the unconditional. Some promises required Israel to do certain things, others Israel can't break if they tried. In this case, the grace leaves as the people reject God by their choice.

> *And I said unto them, If ye think good, give me my price; and if not, forbear. So they weighed for my price thirty pieces of silver.*
> Zechariah 11:12

Exodus 21:32 reveals thirty pieces of silver as the price of a slave.

> *And the Lord said unto me, Cast it unto the potter—a lordly price that I was prized at of them. And I took the thirty pieces of silver, and cast them to the potter in the house of the Lord.*
> Zechariah 11:13

Matthew 27 notes this as being from Jeremiah.

> *Then Judas, which had betrayed him, when he saw that he was condemned, repented himself, and brought again the thirty pieces of silver to the chief priests and elders, Saying, I have sinned in that I have betrayed the innocent blood.*
>
> *And they said, What is that to us? see thou to that. And he cast down the pieces of silver in the temple, and departed, and went and hanged himself.*
>
> *And the chief priests took the silver pieces, and said, It is not lawful for to put them into the treasury, because it is the price of blood. And they took counsel, and bought with them the potter's field, to bury strangers in. Wherefore that field was called, The field of blood, unto this day. Then was fulfilled that which was spoken by Jeremiah the prophet, saying, And they took the thirty pieces of silver, the price of him that was valued, whom they of the children of Israel did value; And gave them for the potter's field, as the Lord appointed me.* Matthew 27:3–10

The scrolls were commonly labeled with the name of the first book, and labeled the scroll with the prophets "Jeremiah." It's just their reference system.

Regarding Judas, he wasn't a shifty-eyed villain as they trusted him with the money. It's common for people to portray Judas as an obvious villain, but he wasn't so. At the last supper, when Jesus reveals one of them will betray Him, they all ask who it is. They didn't all jump up and yell "It's Judas!" Apostates can be missed. They certainly don't *want* to be discovered as such, so they're good at hiding.

> *Then I cut asunder mine other staff, even Bands, that I might break the brotherhood between Judah and Israel.*
> Zechariah 11:14

Since Israel rejects their shepherd we'll see another shepherd appear. Nature abhors a vacuum, so if people reject truth, false ideas always rush in to fill the void. It's your choice to accept or reject it, but never forget truth isn't a popularity contest, truth is what it is.

Here's an instance of a place in the Bible where a large period appears between verses. The first 14 verses involve the Jews rejection of Jesus at His first coming, and in verse 15 we jump to the tribulation. What occurs between verse 14 and verse 15? The church age.

How do we know? Reference Daniel's 70 weeks as an interval of at least 2,000 years occurs between the 69th week and the 70th week. If you haven't studied Daniel and the famous 70 week prophecy, you should as it forms the foundation for all future prophecy. Mistakes made in Daniel carry over into Revelation and cause problems. Do your homework.

> *And the Lord said unto me, Take unto thee yet the instruments of a foolish shepherd.* Zechariah 11:15

Obviously in contrast to the true shepherd. People look for what they want to see, not what is true. If you're in that camp, it's easy to be deceived (fortunately you're not).

> *For, lo, I will raise up a shepherd in the land, which shall not visit those that be cut off, neither shall seek the young one, nor heal that that is broken, nor feed that that standeth still, but he shall eat the flesh of the fat, and tear their claws in pieces.* Zechariah 11:16

The good shepherd discarded and sold for 30 pieces of silver.

People against Christ sometimes imitate His characteristics in an attempt to fool those sincerely seeking Christ, while others take the opposite characteristics to ensnare those who positively don't want to follow Christ; Satan covers all the bases in an attempt to fool as many as possible.

One thing to take away; notice Satan doesn't have any particular idea he wants you to accept. It's not as though he's providing an alternative to God, rather his only goal is to move you away from God. What alternative that might be he cares not.

> *Woe to the idol shepherd that leaveth the flock! The sword shall be upon his arm, and upon his right eye; his arm shall be completely dried up, and his right eye shall be utterly darkened.* Zechariah 11:17

The shepherd should keep watch with his eyes, and use his arms to protect the sheep. This guy can't do that — he's an impostor in place of the true shepherd. We know him as Antichrist, but that actually means in place of.

Too many people look for Antichrist, and Chuck Missler notes we should be talking about the marriage supper of the lamb and the question, do they serve seconds? Who will I be seated next to? If it's Jeremiah, and he asks what I thought of his book, will I be able to respond? Yet another reason to be diligent in your study of God's Word. Do you want to be ducking Zechariah for all eternity?

CHAPTER XVI

Zechariah: Second Coming of Christ

ALTHOUGH ZECHARIAH WROTE ABOUT FUTURE EVENTS, in this section (12–14) the events remain still future and presents another nail in the coffin of the idea God is through with Israel, as this section obviously involves the Jews, and definitely hasn't happened yet.

> *The burden of the word of the Lord for Israel, saith the Lord, who stretcheth forth the heavens, and layeth the foundation of the earth, and formeth the spirit of man within him.*
>
> Zechariah 12:1

It's a bit off-topic, but notice Zechariah makes statements about the Lord creating the universe. It's not from the goo to the zoo to you as evolution isn't even credible science. If you remember your science class in High School, you know science requires something called the scientific method, meaning you make a guess about something, and then perform experiments to prove or disprove your guess. If evolution is science, show the repeatable, peer-reviewed experimental data for the following:

- Matter comes from nothing
- Explosions produce order
- Life comes from non-life

If any *one* of those lack experimental data, you don't have science as all are prerequisites for evolution. Supporters will try to tell you evolution isn't concerned with these, but that means they're ignoring the foundation and trying to build a skyscraper starting with the 10th floor. Doesn't work well for buildings, and doesn't work well for science. Evolution isn't science, it's philosophy.

> *Behold, I will make Jerusalem a cup of trembling unto all the people round about, when they shall be in the siege both against Judah and against Jerusalem.* Zechariah 12:2

In the future, Jerusalem will create problems for all the nations of the world. Even today, what occupies foreign policy? What you do in the Middle East. And then there's Jerusalem; countries all over the globe stay awake at night wondering how to solve the Middle East problem, with Jerusalem at the focus.

The problem isn't the size of Israel, but the existence. It's not possible to swap land for peace as long as one side desires to exterminate the other. The same problem exists with Israel as with abortion. You either terminate a baby or you don't — you can't terminate half a baby. It's a binary operation.

If abortion is right, it's right, and if wrong, it's wrong, but when someone says they're not pro-abortion, but want to reduce the number, they're telling you they're for abortion. You can't fudge out some strange middle position because none exists; anyone stating anything different displays for the world their lack of logic and critical thinking skills.

The same binary problem exists with Israel. If someone wants to exterminate you, how do you work out a compromise? Only exterminate half? Until groups move away from their desire to eliminate all the Jews (not a new idea anyway) compromise isn't possible, because it's a binary operation — either you let the Jews exist or not. Negotiations for peace can't be possible until everyone recognizes Israel's right to exist, and since that hasn't happened yet, you can't get anything done.

Since we're discussing future events, the siege Zechariah mentions hasn't happened yet, but it will.

> *And in that day will I make Jerusalem a burdensome stone for all peoples; all that burden themselves with it shall be cut in pieces, though all the nations of the earth be gathered together against it.* Zechariah 12:3

For *all* people. The whole world will focus on Jerusalem. That's a strange idea since they don't have many resources, don't have a vital transportation hub. The reason for the conflict is as old as time — the Jews have Israel, and someone else wants it.

All nations will gather against it. If you've followed foreign policy of the United States, you've noticed some presidents backtrack on our support of Israel. At some future point, Israel will stand alone. Many people speculate why the United States will abandon Israel; some say from terrorism, others say it's antisemitism, others from economic collapse. It doesn't matter, and it's all a guess.

At this point, anyone who tries to "solve" the Middle East problem will fail, mainly because they fail to understand the problem — it's the existence of Israel, not the size, causing the problem.

> *In that day, saith the Lord, I will smite every horse with terror, and his rider with madness; and I will open mine eyes upon the house of Judah, and will smite every horse of the people with blindness.* Zechariah 12:4

The attacking army will be struck with confusion. 2 Kings 6 verses 1–17 reveal a glimpse of the real reality. Moving forward to verse 24, you see a real problem as they're under siege. In fact, Samaria is reduced to cannibalism (the siege method being camp outside a city and cut it off, and simply wait for them to run out of food and water). In chapter 7, Elisha declares tomorrow the siege will be over. One guy doesn't believe it, and Elisha says you'll see it but won't eat of it.

Meantime, four starving lepers decide to venture out to the Syrian camp, thinking if they kill us, fine, if not, maybe we can eat and live. Unknown to them, the Lord caused the Syrians to hear a noise of chariots, and they all flee. The lepers eat and drink, and when returning to the city tell the people the Syrians are gone, let's go get some food!

What happened to that unbeliever of Elisha's prophecy? He stood in the gate and people trampled over him to retrieve the food. Elisha's prophecy about both the end of the siege, as well as the bureaucrat's future both came to pass exactly as he said.

The lesson — sure, life can be tough, but when you lean on God's promise, it doesn't matter how it appears now, or what the odds are, or who's aligned against you. If the creator of the universe says it, that's the way it's going to be. After all, it's His sandbox. In that day all nations line up against Israel and it looks hopeless, but they forget the one who keeps Israel neither slumbers or sleeps.

> *And the governors of Judah shall say in their heart, The inhabitants of Jerusalem shall be my strength in the Lord of hosts their God. In that day will I make the governors of Judah like an hearth of fire among the wood, and like a torch of fire in a*

> sheaf; and they shall devour all the people round about, on the right hand and on the left; and Jerusalem shall be inhabited again in her own place, even in Jerusalem. Zechariah 12:5-6

It doesn't matter what it looks like, even if Israel stands alone, they'll survive. You might remember the Yom-Kippor war in October 1973 as enemies catch Israel unprepared on their most holy day. Syrian tanks pour into Israel, with not much in their path. From the Jerusalem Post:

> *A Syrian tank brigade passing through the Rafid Gap turned northwest up a little-used route known as the Tapline Road, which cut diagonally across the Golan. This roadway would prove one of the main strategic hinges of the battle. It led straight from the main Syrian breakthrough points to Nafekh, which was not only the location of Israeli divisional headquarters but the most important crossroads on the Heights.*
> *There was no Israeli unit in the Syrians' path.*
> *Temporary salvation came in the form of a solitary lieutenant, Zvika Greengold of Kibbutz Lohamei Hageta'ot. Unattached to any unit because he was enrolled in a course for company commanders, he hitchhiked to Nafekh and offered his services to a staff officer.*
> *For the next 20 hours, Zvika Force, as he came to be known on the radio net, fought running battles with Syrian tanks...**

Israel has been continually attacked since 1948. At times you wonder how they survive; Zechariah reminds you it's the Lord fighting on their behalf.

> *The Lord also shall save the tents of Judah first, that the glory of the house of David and the glory of the inhabitants of Jerusalem do not magnify themselves against Judah.* Zechariah 12:7

In spite of Jerusalem being so critical, the Lord saves Judah first. Some groups look down on others in the country — in our time some on the political left refer to the "flyover" states in the Midwest that tend to lean right, thus liberals in New York fly to San Francisco and never stop in the "flyover" states. It's a term of disdain and contempt.

---

* http://info.jpost.com/C003/Supplements/30YK/art.23.html (accessed Sep 23, 2011)

In a similar manner, Israel could suffer from the same idea — Jerusalem versus the rest of the country. Even though Jerusalem is important, the Lord deals with Judah first, to avoid the common malady we see so often as a group in one part of the country feels superior to another part.

> *In that day shall the Lord defend the inhabitants of Jerusalem; and he that is feeble among them at that day shall be as David; and the house of David shall be as God, as the angel of the Lord before them.* Zechariah 12:8

The Israeli army today performs some pretty impressive feats. A whole army of giant-killers? Jon Courson said when he was in Israel he saw many of the Army wearing T Shirts saying "Don't worry America, Israel has your back."

> *And it shall come to pass in that day, that I will seek to destroy all the nations that come against Jerusalem.* Zechariah 12:9

We as a country haven't learned this truth as we mess around with the Middle East. If you oppose Israel, you'll lose eventually. It doesn't matter the odds, temporary victories only mask the eventual total defeat; Zechariah makes a quick statement, but for detail you've got to dig out Revelation and other prophecy.

> *And I will pour upon the house of David, and upon the inhabitants of Jerusalem, the spirit of grace and of supplications; and they shall look upon me whom they have pierced, and they shall mourn for him, as one mourneth for his only son, and shall be in bitterness for him, as one that is in bitterness for his firstborn.* Zechariah 12:10

This verse reveals the yet future nature of this section. The Jews missed their Messiah the first time around, but at some point they'll acknowledge their mistake. In the Hebrew text, if you look at an interlinear you see the Hebrew, with the English below. After the "whom" you'll notice two letters not translated, the aleph and the tau. That may not mean much, but in Greek it would be the alpha and omega, as aleph and tau are first and last letters of Hebrew alphabet.

> *In that day shall there be a great mourning in Jerusalem, as the mourning of Hadadrimmon in the valley of Megiddon.* Zechariah 12:11

They'll mourn over missing their Messiah. In Matthew when Pilate said he was innocent of this man's blood, what did the crowd say? His blood be on us and our children. At this point, however, they will finally recognize what's going on.

Mistakes can be costly. To avoid mourning over mistakes, why not avoid them in the first place? Sure, some things are out of your control, but as much as possible select your path carefully and you'll avoid many potholes in the road waiting to trip you.

And the land shall mourn, every family apart; the family of the house of David apart, and their wives apart; the family of the house of Nathan apart, and their wives apart; The family of the house of Levi apart, and their wives apart; the family of Shimei apart, and their wives apart; All the families that remain, every family apart, and their wives apart. Zechariah 12:12-14

David represents the kings, Nathan the prophets, and Levi the priests. It's a long winded way to say it involves everyone, and all sections of society as Israel awakens from their blindness to recognize their Messiah. Each person will understand their mistake.

Another strange idea floats around called "collective salvation," but once again those promoters haven't read the text. No question some areas speak of the nation collectively, but salvation itself (as in salvation from hell) always remains a personal and *individual* choice. Collective salvation ... another heretical idea that should be relegated to the scrap heap of ... well ... heretics.

What are they mourning for? Missing the opportunity. You only have so many opportunities, and you can't get them back. If you're spending time on things you can't change, or spiritually unprofitable activities, you might be missing opportunities.

It's an attitude adjustment we need. Zechariah's message has always been that sure things are tough now, maybe even famine, despair, and doom, but it all works out in the end, so get back in the game. Do we learn from the lesson, or simply be doomed to repeat it? It's your choice, your call. Wisely you must choose, yes.

Zechariah spoke of the first coming of Christ, and like Daniel's 70 weeks, a gap exists. Zechariah skips the church age until the coming of the worthless shepherd, or Antichrist. He then picks up the story again as the Jews find themselves in the tribulation. Don't make the mistake thinking the Bible presents events linearly, as a turn of the page could skip thousands of years.

> *In that day there shall be a fountain opened to the house of David and to the inhabitants of Jerusalem for sin and for uncleanness.*
> Zechariah 13:1

"In that day" means the day of the Lord, or the tribulation. What is the purpose of the tribulation? To wake up a nation. It's then they'll realize they missed their Messiah the first time.

If you look back to Ezekiel 37 and the valley of dry bones, Israel may be back in the land right now, but they're basically secular. The dry bones came back to life, but notice in verse 8 while the bones have flesh and muscle, they have no breath in them.

If you understand breath represents the spirit, you also notice Israel isn't exactly following the Lord *spiritually* today. Right now they may be back in the land as a nation, but they're not a spiritual nation quite yet; one reason for the tribulation is to wake up the nation of Israel and return them where they should be.

Who are the house of David and inhabitants of Jerusalem? The Jews, thus they still have a future. In that day they'll be cleansed. Recall Daniel's 70 weeks (Daniel 9) — "to finish the transgression, and to make an end of sins, and to make reconciliation for iniquity, and to bring in everlasting righteousness." Daniel's prophecy could only be about the Jews, and it's obviously never occurred, thus clearly anyone claiming the church replaced Israel hasn't read Daniel's 70 weeks.

Chapters 12–14 of Zechariah will make *no* sense if you don't take it literally; when Zechariah mentions Jerusalem, it means Jerusalem. Those believing the church replaced Israel must play serious Biblical twister to make it imply something other than what it clearly says. Sadly, many people exist who will entertain just such ideas.

> *And it shall come to pass in that day, saith the Lord of hosts, that I will cut off the names of the idols out of the land, and they shall no more be remembered; and also I will cause the prophets and the unclean spirit to pass out of the land.*
> Zechariah 13:2

Idols? Surely we don't have idols anymore, right? Au contraire, mon ami (French for on the contrary, my friend, or as Lee Corso says "Not so fast, my friend"). The *statue* may not exist much anymore, but rest assured, the idols themselves still do.

- Ashtoreth — Pleasure and sexuality. It's good for me, and it doesn't matter who gets hurt as long as my needs are met.
- Baal — Power. Looking at any recent presidential race proves many still worship Baal.
- Mammon — Money. Greed runs rampant in society as everyone from Wall Street to politicians' paybacks to various groups. Nothing is ever enough.
- Molech — Practicality. Molech existed as a statue with arms outstretched and worshipers built a fire in his belly until he glowed red-hot; the idea if you sacrificed your first child Molech would honor your sacrifice and bless you. Surely we don't do such hideous acts today? Today we use salt water instead of fire and call it planned parenthood (sacrificing your first child allows a better career to provide for your next child).
- Nebo — God of knowledge and wisdom. Look at academia and you'll find many still worshiping this ancient god.

These weren't necessarily idols Israel worshiped, but it's a good reminder of what *we* might face. Idolatry remains one of those ancient problems still plaguing us today, even if statues don't inhabit many homes. Some people keep their idols in their heart, hoping nobody will notice, but the Lord always sees, and sometimes He lets people in on the secret.

> *And he brought me to the door of the court; and when I looked, behold a hole in the wall. Then said he unto me, Son of man, dig now in the wall and when I had digged in the wall, behold a door. And he said unto me, Go in, and behold the wicked abominations that they do here.*
>
> *So I went in and saw; and behold every form of creeping things, and abominable beasts, and all the idols of the house of Israel, portrayed upon the wall round about. And there stood before them seventy men of the ancients of the house of Israel, and in the midst of them stood Jaazaniah the son of Shaphan, with every man his censer in his hand; and a thick cloud of incense went up.*
>
> *Then said he unto me, Son of man, hast thou seen what the ancients of the house of Israel do in the dark, every man in the*

chambers of his imagery? For they say, The Lord seeth us not; the Lord hath forsaken the earth. He said also unto me, Turn yet again, and thou shalt see greater abominations that they do.

Then he brought me to the door of the gate of the Lord's house which was toward the north; and, behold, there sat women weeping for Tammuz. Then said he unto me, Hast thou seen this, O son of man? Turn yet again, and thou shalt see greater abominations than these.

And he brought me into the inner court of the Lord's house, and, behold, at the door of the temple of the Lord, between the porch and the altar, were about five and twenty men, with their backs toward the temple of the Lord, and their faces toward the east; and they worshiped the sun toward the east. Ezekiel 8:7-16

Man has problems with idolatry — maybe not a statue, but idols nonetheless. Even Bob Dylan realized you gotta serve somebody — it may be the Lord, or it may be the Devil, but you gotta serve somebody.

And it shall come to pass, that when any shall yet prophesy, then his father and his mother that begat him shall say unto him, Thou shalt not live; for thou speakest lies in the name of the Lord; and his father and his mother that begat him shall thrust him through when he prophesieth. Zechariah 13:3

Tough words, but what standard does a prophet of God have? 100% correct — a bit higher than the National Enquirer. Flip back to Jeremiah 28 for an example of false prophets — those false prophets may sound good and speak the lingo, but they're deceivers. It doesn't matter if they're best selling authors, have big churches or tell you things you want to hear. If it doesn't line up with the Bible, they're heretics.

The only question for those heretics — do they *know* they're peddling lies (in which case they're trying to deceive you) or are they Biblically unaware of what they speak of (in which case they should sit down and do some studying). Either way they're dangerous to your spiritual life.

How serious are we today? Do we tolerate such abominations? That's not to say we should run people through, but in the desire to "fit in" culturally, or be "seeker friendly" some groups abandon the solid rock of the Word of God.

Review chapter 1 and Zechariah's call to repentance. How often do we tolerate idolatry and false teachers? Are we repentant if we tolerate heresy in the church? Or is the pathetic lack of Biblical knowledge in the church causing it to rot from within?

> *And it shall come to pass in that day, that the prophets shall be ashamed every one of his vision, when he hath prophesied; neither shall they wear a rough garment to deceive, But he shall say, I am no prophet, I am a farmer; for man taught me to keep cattle from my youth.* Zechariah 13:4-5

The false prophets will always become known; you can fool some of the people some of the time, but not all of the people all of the time. Just because an idea is popular doesn't mean it's right. Today we're seeing some of the church fooled into abandoning God's Word. For some of you this may once again be something you've never heard of, but rest assured some of those calling themselves "Christians" (and yes, we use the term *very* loosely) abandon such basic doctrine as the inerrancy of the Bible, the resurrection of Jesus, the gospel, sin, and more. Consider *one* case in which traditional, orthodox Christianity becomes replaced by social justice, good works, and philosophy.

> *Within the evangelical world, tensions have emerged between those who deny secular knowledge, and those who have kept up with it and integrated it with their faith. ... We find students arriving on campus tired of the culture-war approach to faith in which they were raised, and more interested in promoting social justice than opposing gay marriage.*
>
> *They understand that Christian theology can incorporate Darwin's insights and flourish in a pluralistic society.*[*]

First off, a pluralistic society is an oxymoron. Plural is, well, plural, while a society is singular. Right up front statements like this make everyone ooh and ahh (my, look how scholarly they sound), but as soon as you try and figure out what they're saying you'll discover they've done nothing but string together buzzwords, almost as if they picked them from shooting darts.

In any event, scientists want, you know, actual *science*. Evolution science? There's an oxymoron. Where is the repeatable, scientific, experimental evidence for the following?

---

[*] http://www.nytimes.com/2011/10/18/opinion/the-evangelical-rejection-of-reason.html (accessed Dec 30, 2011)

- Matter coming from nothing.
- Goo becoming alive.

A lack of actual science could be one reason why so many become duped by Piltdown man and other hoaxes fostered on the scientific community. They already hold preconceived ideas of what they want, and then grasp at anything that might prove their guess. Like Wile E. Coyote their theories eventually plummet to the rocks below in a huge "poof." We don't need trendy "integration" with mans' wisdom. It's not about trendy or popular, but *what is true*. The church tried rule by people instead of God, and it didn't turn out very well.

> *And unto the angel of the church of the Laodiceans write ... Because thou sayest, I am rich, and increased with goods, and have need of nothing; and knowest not that thou art wretched, and miserable, and poor, and blind, and naked ... As many as I love, I rebuke and chasten; be zealous therefore, and repent. Behold, I stand at the door, and knock; if any man hear my voice, and open the door, I will come in to him, and will sup with him, and he with me.*   Revelation 3

Laodicea roughly means "rule of the people," or perhaps we could call it "integrating secular knowledge" via popular opinion. The people are in charge, not God or inerrant scripture. Where is Jesus in this church? Outside trying to get in. How did it work out for them? Notice Jesus has *nothing* good to say about them. Also notice they thought they were in great shape, but Jesus points out their real condition was the opposite of what they thought — they were living in delusion.

Be a skeptic. False prophets — of either the religious *or* science type — have a way of being found out, but unfortunately looooong after many become victimized by them. Be a skeptic and do your own research, and you'll find much of what you've been told turns out to be false.

> *And one shall say unto him, What are these wounds in thine hands? Then he shall answer, Those with which I was wounded in the house of my friends.*   Zechariah 13:6

We shift to Jesus, as the Jewish people finally recognize what they've been waiting for all these years.

> *Awake, O sword, against my shepherd, and against the man that is my fellow, saith the Lord of hosts; smite the shepherd, and the sheep shall be scattered; and I will turn mine hand upon the little ones.* Zechariah 13:7

After Jesus was crucified, it wasn't long after the Jewish people were scattered abroad, and didn't come back until the 1940's.

> *And it shall come to pass, that in all the land, saith the Lord, two parts therein shall be cut off and die; but the third shall be left therein.* Zechariah 13:8

Two-thirds killed? "Never again" may be a theme, but Zechariah says only one-third survive. Read Revelation; it's a pretty rough time for anyone on the earth — you don't want to be here during that time.

Why have the Jewish people been so attacked through the years? First, because if the Jews didn't exist, it means the Messiah couldn't arrive. After that, why? Some believe a prerequisite for Jesus' return is for the Jews to *ask* for the Messiah to return, and acknowledge their sin (Matthew 23:37–39 and Hosea 5:15). If that's true, then if the Jewish people aren't around, it means Jesus can't return, thus explaining the continued attacks by Satan to destroy them.

> *And I will bring the third part through the fire, and will refine them as silver is refined, and will test them as gold is tested; they shall call on my name, and I will hear them. I will say, It is my people; and they shall say, The Lord is my God.* Zechariah 13:9

The Jews are God's people. It's clear God isn't through with the Jewish people (connect Ezekiel 37+, Daniel 9, Zechariah 12–14, and Revelation), and they still have a major role to play.

As we move into the final chapter (no pun intended) of history, some take this as allegory or already fulfilled history in some sense, but we'll take it as it reads — a prophetic account of future events to be literally fulfilled as Zechariah reminds us life may be tough right now, but look what the future holds. Some of this requires very little commentary as it's clear. You only need extensive comments if you ignore what the text clearly says, as J Vernon McGee says:

If you are wanting to know the position of a pastor whom you're not sure about, if you want to know what he believes, take the fourteenth chapter of Zechariah to him and ask him to explain it to you. You will find out what a man really believes when he deals with this chapter.*

Later we'll cover post-modern philosophy in depth, but in brief it denies absolutes — value relativism. Simply put, if you don't like what the Bible says, change the meaning by either allegorizing it away, or claiming that part doesn't apply today. That doesn't work out, but many try it anyway. In this case, notice Zechariah doesn't make a qualified statement. It can't be stopped.

Behold, the day of the Lord cometh, and thy spoil shall be divided in the midst of thee. Zechariah 14:1

Hebrew days begin at sunset — the dark. The day of the Lord begins in the darkness of the Tribulation, and ends in the brightness of the second coming of Christ.

For I will gather all nations against Jerusalem to battle; and the city shall be taken, and the houses rifled, and the women ravished; and half of the city shall go forth into captivity, and the residue of the people shall not be cut off from the city.
Zechariah 14:2

Chuck Missler calls all nations the "United Nations" as a pun, but it could be, as all means all. That implies the United States abandons Israel as well (which isn't a surprise if you follow presidential actions).

Who speaks here? The Lord Himself as He scripts these final events. What do you suppose the people of Jerusalem think at this time? It's all over, we're doomed. God abandoned us, etc. That's not an uncommon feeling, either in the Bible or for us today. It's always darkest in the middle of the night, when *you* see no way out. Remember, this begins in the night — despair, gloom, and doubt — and ends in light — the return of Christ.

Then shall the Lord go forth, and fight against those nations, as when he fought in the day of battle. Zechariah 14:3

The Lord fought for Israel many times in the past.

---
*   McGee (1982, page 984)

- Red Sea vs Egypt — they had no hope, with their backs against the wall.
- Jericho — the most bizarre battle plan ever.
- My favorite, Gideon in Judges 7.

As the Lord has done in the past, so He will now do as He defends Israel.

And his feet shall stand in that day upon the mount of Olives, which is before Jerusalem on the east, and the mount of Olives shall cleave in the midst thereof toward the east and toward the west, and there shall be a very great valley; and half of the mountain shall remove toward the north, and half of it toward the south. Zechariah 14:4

For those post-modernists allegorizing this chapter, did Jesus exist? The Mount of Olives? Jerusalem? So for what reason would you say this verse means anything other than what it says? It's clearly no figure of speech. The only reason someone might claim otherwise is they simply reject what the text says, but want to call themselves "Christian." George Orwell called that doublethink, or the idea of holding conflicting ideas at the same time, and defending both.

And ye shall flee to the valley of the mountains; for the valley of the mountains shall reach unto Azel; yea, ye shall flee, like as ye fled from before the earthquake in the days of Uzziah king of Judah; and the Lord my God shall come, and all the saints with thee. And it shall come to pass in that day, that the light shall not be clear, nor dark, But it shall be one day which shall be known to the Lord, not day, nor night; but it shall come to pass, that at evening time it shall be light. Zechariah 14:5-7

The earthquake does more than shake the earth. It apparently alters the environment.

And it shall be in that day, that living waters shall go out from Jerusalem; half of them toward the former sea, and half of them toward the hinder sea, in summer and in winter shall it be. Zechariah 14:8

It could be the earthquake did much more than shake the earth. If it moves the axis of the earth it could return the earth to a more even temperate climate over the entire globe, much like the equator is now, with no more extremes of winter and summer. It's likely much more exists in verses 6–8 than we can guess.

> *And the Lord shall be king over all the earth; in that day shall there be one Lord, and his name one.*   Zechariah 14:9

It doesn't seem that way now, as evil and chaos has its way, but that's only a temporary situation.

> *All the land shall be turned as a plain from Geba to Rimmon south of Jerusalem; and it shall be lifted up, and inhabited in its place, from Benjamin's gate unto the place of the first gate, unto the corner gate, and from the tower of Hananeel unto the king's winepresses. And men shall dwell in it, and there shall be no more utter destruction; but Jerusalem shall be safely inhabited.*   Zechariah 14:10-11

Jerusalem isn't necessarily safe today. But then it will be.

> *And this shall be the plague with which the Lord will smite all the people that have fought against Jerusalem; Their flesh shall consume away while they stand upon their feet, and their eyes shall consume away in their holes, and their tongue shall consume away in their mouth.*   Zechariah 14:12

Notice that fought appears in the past tense. You should recall way back in Genesis "And I will bless them that bless thee, and curse him that curseth thee" — those fighting against Israel have no chance of succeeding in the long term.

This verse mentions some strange weapons, perhaps a neutron bomb — the idea being to destroy the people without destroying much property. It's intense radiation with not as much explosion designed to defeat armored vehicles and personnel, causing flesh to melt away. It's certainly possible Zechariah could refer to some new weapon we haven't seen yet, but a neutron bomb fits the description quite well.

You hear the phrase "let's not be on the wrong side of history," usually as supporting some radical cause. Yet we don't mind being on the wrong side of the future as the country abandons Israel. Doesn't make sense. *All* the people who fight against Jerusalem share this fate? We definitely (individually or as a nation) don't want to be in that group.

> *And it shall come to pass in that day, that a great tumult from the Lord shall be among them; and they shall lay hold every one on the hand of his neighbor, and his hand shall rise up against the hand of his neighbor. And Judah also shall fight*

> *at Jerusalem; and the wealth of all the nations round about shall be gathered together, gold, and silver, and apparel, in great abundance. And so shall be the plague of the horse, of the mule, of the camel, and of the donkey, and of all the beasts that shall be in these tents, as this plague.*
>
> *And it shall come to pass, that every one that is left of all the nations which came against Jerusalem shall even go up from year to year to worship the King, the Lord of hosts, and to keep the feast of tabernacles.* Zechariah 14:13-16

For those trying to provide alternate ideas for this chapter — if you cling to any possibility this chapter has been fulfilled or is historical, can you explain when this ever happened? We thought so, as another strange idea bites the dust. Those that are left after doing battle with the Lord finally heed the subtle clue, and figure out who the true God is.

> *And it shall be, that whoever will not come up of all the families of the earth unto Jerusalem to worship the King, the Lord of hosts, even upon them shall be no rain.* Zechariah 14:17

Those rebelling will have some motivation. As we see in Revelation, some people are so hard-hearted even in the face of clear and compelling events by God, they still reject the idea of God.

> *And if the family of Egypt go not up, and come not, that have no rain; there shall be the plague, with which the Lord will smite the nations that come not up to keep the feast of tabernacles. This shall be the punishment of Egypt, and the punishment of all nations that come not up to keep the feast of tabernacles.* Zechariah 14:18-19

Egypt provides another example of people who fail to learn the lessons of history and thus end up repeating them. Remember Moses guys? Last time you went up against the Lord it didn't end well. Learn the lesson the first time, then you don't have to repeat the class.

> *In that day shall there be upon the bells of the horses, HOLINESS UNTO THE Lord; and the pots in the Lord's house shall be like the bowls before the altar. Yea, every pot in Jerusalem and in Judah shall be holiness unto the Lord of hosts; and all they that sacrifice shall come and take of them, and boil in them; and in that day there shall be no more the Canaanite in the house of the Lord of hosts.* Zechariah 14:20-21

All will be dedicated to the Lord. Public life (horses), religious life (Lord's house), and private life.

Zechariah ends with the final encouragement for the people — get back in the game, finish the job, run the race. Sure it looks hard now, but see the future. Maybe that's no good for you, you feel more like Rocky after twelve rounds with Apollo Creed. It's past being on the ropes. Maybe doubting God totally, and maybe a bit mad. Let's be honest, and not be Tony the Tiger Christians (where everything is grrrrrrrreat!).

You're not alone, as even the giant of the New Testament felt that way when writing to Corinth — Paul.

> *For we would not, brethren, have you ignorant of our trouble which came to us in Asia, that we were pressed out of measure, above strength, insomuch that we despaired even of life*
> 2 Corinthians 1:8

As Zechariah 14 shows, God allows or creates situations just to show His power. Does that mean you'll understand? Maybe, maybe not. When your back's against the wall, when you're on the ropes, when it's fourth and long ... then what?

In Judges chapter 7 Gideon waits to attack, but the Lord stops him and says you've got too many men Gideon. What? Too many men? In battle, you can never have enough. Nevertheless, the Lord trims the number down quite a bit before the attack, and then tells Gideon, go get 'em.

What's that got to do with what you're going through now? Quite a bit actually, as the answer comes from Judges 7.

> *And the Lord said unto Gideon, The people that are with thee are too many for me to give the Midianites into their hands, lest Israel vaunt themselves against me, saying, Mine own hand hath saved me.*
> Judges 7:2

The same principle applies to us. The best counselors, advisors, friends, pastor, and all else. When all that fails, perhaps that's the Lord saying to you as He did to Gideon — you've got too many men, and if you rely on them, you'll boast about how your own plans and actions saved you.

Romans 8:28 says all things work together for good. *All* things, not some; it also doesn't say we'll see it, or understand it. And that's a good thing, because most of the time I don't.

Refuse to quit — no plan B exists. There's no great solution sometimes, no magic words to make it feel better, no great understanding coming. You see the end, it won't always be the way it is now, no matter what it seems like. How we travel from now to Zechariah 14 I have no idea, but I do know we'll arrive there.

Recall Daniel's three friends standing before the king after they refuse the King's order, as he says "BOW OR BURN," and those three Hebrew youths reply to the king:

> *O Nebuchadnezzar, we are not careful to answer thee in this matter. If it be so, our God whom we serve is able to deliver us from the burning fiery furnace, and he will deliver us out of thine hand, O king. But if not, be it known unto thee, O king, that we will not serve thy gods, nor worship the golden image which thou hast set up.* Daniel 3:16–18

We can't quit, we can't serve foreign gods, we can't yield. Sometimes being stubborn is a *good* thing, even though it's tough. Those three guys refused to quit, and they provide a summation of all that Zechariah tried to relate to us — sure, it's tough now, and might even look hopeless, but put me in coach, I'm ready to play!

One reason to become involved with skeptics and critics is so when those 3 AM times come, when it's really dark, when you're beyond your ability to endure, when all is stripped away, you can be much more confident of what the Bible says, after spending so much time with people trying to prove it wrong and they've all come up empty. I'm sure they'll keep trying, just as Wile E. Coyote knows *this* time ACME Corporation's gadget will finally work and he'll capture the Road Runner (then again, maybe not).

CHAPTER XVII

The Problem

MANY CHRISTIANS EXIST IN A SAD state — not really thriving, yet not totally carnal either. They may be saved, but they certainly haven't entered the abundant life Jesus promised. Just as the Jews exited Egypt (the world), they arrive at the promised land but refuse to enter.

Many people say the promised land represents heaven, but that's not exactly right for a simple reason — many battles still exist. So what does the promised land represent? The abundant, spirit-filled life Jesus promised. You're not *forced* to enter, you must *want* to.

Unfortunately, just like the Jews, many Christians fail to learn the lesson, wandering in the wilderness instead of entering the promised land victorious. Why? We've watched too many infomercials promising rock-hard abs with no exercise required (but wait! If you call now, we'll send the super-special diet drink guaranteeing massive weight loss, while letting you eat hot dogs and ice cream).

Results require effort, sometimes hard effort. In short, we're slackers, stuck at a beginner white belt while fooling ourselves into believing we're seasoned black belts. Is it any wonder the church became so anemic? We've raised a generation of pew-warmers instead of trained combat veterans.

The real problem comes from people wanting to live an easy, carefree life instead of doing their duty. Duty? Whoops, that's one of those words we don't hear anymore — duty, honor, commitment, integrity. Before the mob arrives, please note everyone has flaws, everyone makes mistakes (it's not about being perfect). But how hard do you try to live up to the goal? Hint: read Psalm 15 for the Biblical view.

Since those attitudes have long passed in business, marriage, and day to day life, should it surprise us those attitudes (or lack thereof) infect the church? It's *easier* to go back to Egypt than to venture into the spirited adventure of the promised land. While it flows with blessings, giants exist to be defeated, and if you're not prepared, well, let's just say it won't end well (yes, it's the pig image again).

Thus, many people prefer the bondage of Egypt (slavery) over what God promised. Where is the abundant life He promised? Just like the Jews leaving Egypt, it's yours for the taking *if you're willing to fight for it.* Or you can return to the bondage in Egypt and receive three squares a day, along with making bricks for Pharaoh. Your choice, your call, but we can't help but be reminded of the Samuel Adams quote we've noted before.

> *If ye love wealth greater than liberty, the tranquility of servitude greater than the animating contest for freedom, go home from us in peace. We seek not your counsel, nor your arms. Crouch down and lick the hand that feeds you; May your chains set lightly upon you, and may posterity forget that ye were our countrymen.* ~ Samuel Adams

That's not perfectly applicable to our situation, but you get the idea. Understand this: if you choose to enter the promised land, it's rough, and don't be surprised when the enemy fights back. You'd better be prepared and combat-ready, because if you're not it won't end well.

How can people who sit in church decade after decade fail when problems arise? How can (as we've seen happen) wives leave their husbands for Internet flings? I used to think when hearing of such things those people weren't grounded or became victims of poor teaching, but I've since changed my mind after seeing people with decades under quality teaching go sideways.

Why?

For some reason, people have a difficult time *applying* what they *know*. It's because they've not availed themselves of proper training — they're still beginner white belts, despite years of what they call training. It's time to change that, and progress from beginner (what Paul called the milk of the Word) to the meat. Sure, it's tough, and you'll likely be dinged along the way. After all, Christianity requires a full-contact combat lifestyle and mindset.

For various reasons we'll ignore, people have learned to compartmentalize life — this is the "God" box, this is the "work" box, this is the "social" box, and so on. Thus, in one box they can lie to their spouse and drink at the bar, meetup on the Internet, and so on, all the while believing in their heart they're not doing anything wrong.

How? They've separated the "God" Box from the "work" box, from the "wife" box, and so on. Things that would never happen in the "God" box are welcomed in the "work" box. Think this is crazy? It's Chuck Missler saying "never underestimate a person's ability to rationalize"; a rationalizing person attends church on Sunday while secretly cheating on their wife or being a closet alcoholic.

A great discovery awaits you: Christianity not only works on Sunday but every day — it's how you live your life, as University of Oregon basketball player Luke Ridnour discovered.

> ... along with Ridnour's successes also came defeats and frustrations. ... "If I played well, I was up. If I played down, I was down. So, everything I accomplished was how I was on the court. I didn't have a way out. I never had peace, so I started to search that out."
>
> "When I started reading the Word, everything changed — the way I thought, the way I acted, my attitude." And with that, for the first time in his life, basketball was not the first thing in his life.*

To paraphrase Zechariah — not by slogan, nor by feelings, but by my spirit, saith the Lord.

Sure, you're saved, but does it make an impact? Can you sit and listen for years, failing to put in practice what you know to be true? It's time to break down the boxes and realize it's *all* God's box; you must make your relationship with God more than an emergency thing ("in case of emergency break glass"). It's how you live, breathe, and get out of bed.

We've got to match our perception with reality. Too many Christians walk around thinking they're a 30-year black belt, when in reality they're nothing more than a white belt who never advanced. Much of what you need in life you'll learn in martial arts — perseverance, integrity, honor, hard work.

---

*   "Oregon Quarterly" Summer 2011, page 46

We'll lay the groundwork you'll require to fix this problem, then see examples of the principles in action, and finally (hopefully) figure out how to apply them to your Christian life.

Nobody simply *hands* you the next level belt because you've been in class for a certain time (for those of you from a public school background this concept may be foreign to you, but that's a topic for another book). No, you have to *earn* your rank, with sweat, hard work, and dedication. If you've been training for years, but never earned the next level belt, do you think you could match up with someone who's trained for the same time, but earned black belt status? In short, you're in big trouble (the pig makes a comeback ... again).

It's time for Christians to move past beginner status.

CHAPTER XVIII

It's a Battle Out There

A DEBATE ABOUT WHETHER SATAN REALLY exists or not ran on ABC News. Sadly, some religious people deny the existence of Satan, believing Satan exists only as a product of our imagination or as a result of mental illness. Apparently, they've never had to oppose him.

Those people simply fail to have a correct view of reality, instead choosing to live in delusion. They *wished* for a certain thing, and convinced themselves it would actually come about (and I want a pony too). Unfortunately, they're absolutely wrong as the cosmos we inhabit isn't the real reality; physicists tell us the world we inhabit actually consists of other dimensions.

Just because we can't observe other dimensions in our daily life doesn't make them less real. It's nice of the physicists to catch up to the Bible, as the Bible understood multi-dimensional space thousands of years ago.

> *Then the king of Syria warred against Israel, and took counsel with his servants, saying, In such and such a place shall be my camp. And the man of God sent unto the king of Israel, saying, Beware that thou pass not such a place; for there the Syrians are come down. And the king of Israel sent to the place which the man of God told him and warned him of, and saved himself there, not once nor twice.* 2 Kings 6:8-10

The king thinks he's got a spy in his inner circle, as the king of Israel always seems to know his plans, but his servants explain what's going on.

> *Therefore the heart of the king of Syria was very troubled for this thing; and he called his servants, and said unto them, Will ye not show me which of us is for the king of Israel? And one of his servants said, None, my lord, O king; but Elisha, the prophet that is in Israel, telleth the king of Israel the words that thou speakest in thy bedchamber.*   2 Kings 6:11-12

If you're the king, what do you do? You send a military squad out to find Elisha and eliminate him.

> *And he said, Go and spy where he is, that I may send and fetch him. And it was told him, saying, Behold, he is in Dothan. Therefore sent he there horses, and chariots, and a great host; and they came by night, and compassed the city about.*   2 Kings 6:13-14

Problem solved, at least the king thinks. Of course, as Doc from the "Back to the Future" movies stated repeatedly "you're not thinking fourth-dimensionally." His plan worked perfectly, at least from the human perspective, as Elisha's servant wakes up and looks outside.

> *And when the servant of the man of God was risen early, and gone forth, behold, an host compassed the city both with horses and chariots. And his servant said unto him, Alas, my master! What shall we do?*   2 Kings 6:15

Poor guy wakes up in a panic! Elisha doesn't seem too worried about it, telling the servant they that are with us are more than they that are with them. Naturally, the servant doesn't get it, and (what's not in the Bible) continually pesters Elisha about it. Elisha realizes he's not going to get any sleep until he solves the servant's little problem, so he asks God to let the servant in on the secret.

> *And Elisha prayed, and said, Lord, I pray thee, open his eyes, that he may see. And the Lord opened the eyes of the young man; and he saw; and, behold, the mountain was full of horses and chariots of fire round about Elisha.*   2 Kings 6:17

What did the servant see? He saw a window into the multi-dimensional space we inhabit. Elisha knew of its existence, but the servant did only upon seeing it (just because someone doesn't believe something doesn't affect reality).

Do you believe what happens in those other dimensions? Or are you debating whether Satan actually exists or not? If you don't believe in Satan's existence and multi-dimensional space, put the book down and go back to watching re-runs of "Frasier."

Examine your weaponry. Remember, you're fighting in multi-dimensional space, so much of what you think has value doesn't. The classic list appears in Paul's letter to the Ephesians, and we'll take a *brief* look at what God provides. As a serious student, you must train and learn more on your own, as it's all you've got.

Paul first provides an exhortation, saying "Put on the whole armor of God, that ye may be able to stand against the wiles of the devil." Paul speaks in military terms, and since you're already aware of the enemy surrounding you Paul's emphasis should not surprise you. You need *all* you can get, one or two parts won't do. Using what's provided remains the *only* way you can survive. Take this as a command from General Paul: take up the entire weaponry God provides.

BELT OF TRUTH — Paul speaks of girding your waist with truth, phrasing you might not exactly be familiar with. In that day they wore flowing robes, so girding your waist meant to tie up your robe so you would have complete freedom of movement. In other words, be prepared for action!

Our belt is truth. If you pay attention to news today, you'll be amazed at how often you're lied to. Many people don't even try to hide their contempt for you, assuming you'll buy any lies they present. As extra credit for the serious student (and we *all* should be serious students) you'll require training in logic and critical thinking, and a good place to start is "Discerning Truth" by Dr. Jason Lisle*.

BREASTPLATE OF RIGHTEOUSNESS — Proper protection is vital. Many believe this is righteousness God imputes to you when you're saved, but that's not exactly right. Recall back in the opening of the letter Paul writes to Christians, and in this section tells those Christians to pick up the armor. In other words, *you might not have this piece yet.*

So what's Paul mean? Paul speaks of the day-to-day life of integrity and honor you should live by. If you need a refresher, consider Daniel in Daniel 6 as his enemies try to attack him but couldn't find any skeletons in his closet, concluding the only way

---

*   ISBN 978-0890515945

to trap Daniel comes by creating a conflict between man's law and God's.

FOOTGEAR — You'll not get very far without proper footwork. It's important to remain light and agile on your feet. What does Paul say? Preparedness — exactly what we've already talked about as one of the reasons why Christians fail. You will be different. You'll dive in and be prepared, and separate yourself from the masses who wonder — what's happening?

SHIELD OF FAITH — Shields provide a maneuverable protection barrier. Our shield is a shield of faith, and what is that? Perhaps the toughest part to acquire, and may take the longest. This isn't saving faith, it's faith in God's plan, it's confidence.

Recall the disciples on the lake as Jesus and they traveled across when a storm arises. They quickly panic, and wake Jesus up with a "don't you care we're dying?" attitude. Many people think the faith they lacked was not realizing who Jesus was (sort of a saving faith).

Not so for the simple reason *they woke Him up*. If you or I had been in the boat they certainly wouldn't have awakened us. No, they completely understood who was in the boat with them, the faith they lacked was God does what He says — when He says let's go to the other side, He means let's go to the other side.

That doesn't mean the journey will be easy, however.

HELMET OF SALVATION — Once again, you may not have this piece of equipment; it's not a question of *if* you're saved, it's a question of confidence. Many people lack confidence in their salvation, and you'll run across people who believe you can lose your salvation. Not so. If you have those questions, you need to dive in and solve them.

SWORD OF THE SPIRIT — It's become popular Christian-speak to talk about the sword, but too many wave it around wildly and hope they hit something.

Not so with you, you realize the sword (just like the Roman one) provides the most advanced weaponry you can have, but it's useless without continued and advanced training. If you think just because you posses the most advanced weapon you'll survive, well, recall the pig from previous chapters. It's not a pretty picture.

ATTITUDE — You're a soldier. As such, life isn't always easy, or fun. Remember what Paul told Timothy "No man that warreth entangleth himself with the affairs of this life; that he may please him who hath chosen him to be a soldier." If that's your goal, you've got to move off thoughts of a Lexus, and continually ask yourself, how does this impact eternity? If it doesn't, can it be discarded?

That doesn't mean you shouldn't have down time, or never watch TV, but realize the soldier doesn't exist for relaxation, but to move forward in battle. If you've come this far, you realize the reality of what you find yourself in demands the proper attitude, dedication, and commitment.

Your goal at the end of your life should be the same as Paul's — I've fought the good fight, I've finished the course, I've kept the faith.

CHAPTER XIX

The Opposition

IF YOU'RE INVOLVED IN MILITARY CONFLICT, common sense requires you to understand who you're fighting against, and the nature of the adversary. Sadly, many Christians skip this vital first step, and instead of focused and targeted responses, swing wildly above their head hoping they'll hit something, a tactic not well-suited to winning.

19.1 The World

It's no surprise Christians find themselves in conflict with the world, as the world lies under Satan's control — you're essentially behind enemy lines, surrounded by unfriendly entities. Many Christians have no idea their status, and certainly don't like to be advised of it — they're living in delusion.

You've been awakened, and can now look at the world as it actually is. However, the average person has little idea of the true powers behind the world they inhabit, and many of those have no desire to escape the fantasy they dwell in.

Since the majority of the world exhibits either open hostility or apathy towards reality, don't be surprised when you find yourself in the minority against the world's systems. Don't be discouraged, as right and wrong are not found via majority or popular opinion.

Nevertheless, the world's systems have been tuned in an attempt to defeat you if possible, and if not, at the very least discourage or disable you to render you ineffective. If you're not moving forward, you're moving backward — neutrality simply isn't an option. Thus, whether you're defeated, or simply not functioning, the enemy wins.

Today's culture likes to believe man has evolved and cast aside the primitive cultures of the past ("every day in every way we're getting better and better"), but that's not true. Nothing changes, as Solomon said there's nothing new under the sun. Those old pagan gods never left, they're still around today (yes, we've covered these before, but like Peter as long as we're alive we'll continue to remind you of things).

- Ashtoreth — Pleasure and sexuality. It's good for me, and it doesn't matter who gets hurt as long as my needs are met.
- Baal — Power. Looking at any recent presidential race proves many still worship Baal.
- Mammon — Money. Greed runs rampant in society as everyone from Wall Street to politicians' paybacks to various groups. Nothing is ever enough.
- Molech — Practicality. Molech existed as a statue with arms outstretched with worshipers building a fire in his belly until he glowed red-hot; the idea if you sacrificed your first child Molech would honor your sacrifice and bless you. Surely we don't do such hideous acts today? Today we use salt water instead of fire and call it planned parenthood (sacrificing your first child allows a better career to provide for your next child).
- Nebo — God of knowledge and wisdom. Look at academia and you'll find many still worshiping this ancient god.

Oh sure, nobody (well, almost nobody) has a physical idol statue in their house, but as you can see, *all* those ancient gods surround us today; the failure to recognize them causes problems. It's easy to recognize attempts by atheists and other groups trying to stamp out your rights, but those old pagan gods stealthily sneak in to ensnare many.

You must be in the world — and understand its systems — without being *of* the world. We've covered The Matrix earlier, consider how Neo and his companions could go in and out of The Matrix at will (and affect events inside), but were no longer *part* of that system. Attempts to withdraw, or a failure to recognize reality, will both cause problems. As with many things in life, balance is required; extreme views are *usually* wrong. You require an honest and healthy understanding of reality.

In military actions, actionable intelligence gathering about the situation will always be the first priority. If you don't understand the enemy, you can't defeat him. Thus, if you understand the terrain you're fighting on, you're already one step ahead of those blindly entering into combat.

19.2 The Flesh

The flesh can be a generic term to cover several aspects of human existence, or as John said in his first letter:

> *For all that is in the world, the lust of the flesh, and the lust of the eyes, and the pride of life, is not of the Father, but is of the world.* 1 John 2:16

Satan's tactics don't change over the thousands of years man has walked the earth for a simple reason: we have not evolved or grown — the same tricks still trap people today. In fact, the same trick from the garden of Eden still works. Let's look back to the garden and see what Eve's problem was.

> *And when the woman saw that the tree was good for food, and that it was pleasant to the eyes, and a tree to be desired to make one wise, she took of the fruit thereof, and did eat, and gave also unto her husband with her; and he did eat.* Genesis 3:6

Eve saw three things in the forbidden fruit:

1. "the tree was good for food" — the lust of the flesh.
2. "pleasant to the eyes" — lust of the eyes.
3. "desired to make one wise" — pride of life.

Perhaps the biggest problem comes as Chuck Missler says "Never underestimate a persons ability to rationalize," meaning many of these problems we never notice, because it's easy to rationalize them away.

For example, when David killed Bathsheba's husband he certainly didn't view it as murder. It took a prophet to provide David with a story that he *did* recognize as wrong, and then the prophet provided those famous words — "You're the man." Only at that point did David recognize his sin, and repent. Your own attitudes and desires might not be spiritually aligned; don't attempt to rationalize, as Nathan said — you're the man.

19.3 The Devil

You must recognize the world in which you dwell does not provide a hospitable environment. However, Satan doesn't care if you're off on one side or the other, as long as you fail to comprehend the truth. In this case, two common mistakes occur.

1. Satan doesn't exist.
2. Satan lies behind every corner.

Either believing Satan doesn't exist, or he's all powerful and able to beat you are incorrect. Both mistakes cause you to fail in your Christian life. Both mistakes are fine with Satan.

So what's the truth? Satan exists. He's powerful. He's studying you. He likely knows the Bible better than you do. He knows how to push your buttons. He can predict with high probability of success how you'll respond to any situation.

But he can't beat you. No matter what. The only way for the enemy to win is *if you quit*. That's Satan's strategy — to get you to quit. That comes by either failing to acknowledge his reality (in which case there's no reason to fight an imaginary foe), or thinking he's too powerful (in which case it's futile). Either way, Satan wins. You must understand he's a real entity, but subject to God's authority. In the end (as the answers are in the back of the book), what is Satan's end?

> *And the devil that deceived them was cast into the lake of fire and brimstone, where the beast and the false prophet are, and shall be tormented day and night for ever and ever.*
> Revelation 20:10

All through history Satan *knows* his final destiny. He can't win, and he knows it. The question is, do you?

CHAPTER XX

Teamwork

ONE COMMON TRAIT CHRISTIANITY shares with martial arts: you never finish your training, you can always improve. You will *never* arrive at a point you know it all. As Chuck Missler says, the Bible is shallow enough a baby can play in it, but deep enough an elephant can immerse in it. You'll *never* learn it all. You'll change and move beyond what Paul called the milk of the Word to be sure, but you'll never arrive at the end — it's an infinite journey.

Yet Christianity remains a full contact sport. If you're not prepared to dive in and engage, you'll likely become a casualty. Sorry, that's just the way it is. If you're not practicing with the armor of God, you're toast. If you're filled with pride, you'll be disqualified. If you fail to understand the real world and prefer The Matrix, you'll never be effective.

You must put aside those things that are harmful, and embrace those which benefit. Sadly, too many Christians confuse those two lists. Your Lexus won't help you, neither will your PhD, finances, power, or prestige. Additionally, if you're standing on the sidelines you're letting down your fellow soldiers. The church forms a military unit, and to be effective you need to understand the organization of the Marines as they organize by the "rule of threes."

- *Fire Team* — team leader (M4/M16), rifleman (M16), machine gunner (M249), grenadier (M203). Team leader is lance corporal or corporal.
- *Squad* — three fire teams, with corporal or sergeant as squad leader.

- *Rifle Platoon* — three squads, with a platoon leader and a navy corpsman.
- *Rifle Company* — three rifle platoons, weapons platoon, and support staff.
- *Battalion* — three rifle companies and other support.
- *Regiment* — three battalions.
- *Division* — three infantry regiments and an artillery regiment.

How does that relate to the church? Well, no analogy is faultless, but consider the Fire Team the family. Those Fire Teams (at least in New Testament times) organized into small home fellowships (similar to a squad), usually with a leader over them. Squads form city-wide churches, and those churches form the world-wide church, with Christ as the head.

If you fail to understand the military requirements and organization, you'll be ineffective (at best), or a casualty (at worst). Once again, too many Christians fail to understand their role and place in the larger overall church. What happens if your Fire Team drops out, is ineffective, or due to your lack of training and diligence, becomes a casualty? The roles your team *should* handle must be absorbed by other Fire Teams.

Recall our discussion earlier about Samuel Adams?

> *If ye love wealth greater than liberty, the tranquility of servitude greater than the animating contest for freedom, go home from us in peace. We seek not your counsel, nor your arms. Crouch down and lick the hand that feeds you; May your chains set lightly upon you, and may posterity forget that ye were our countrymen.*

You need to be well-trained. Repeat after me: *it's not the pastor's duty to do the work, it's his function to train the rest.* Let that sink in, and keep repeating it. Pew-warmers like to put the burden on the pastor and a small group*, but the church should prepare *you* for work, you should not watch others work (that's yet another problem with the current fad over "social justice," which seeks to transfer individuals' responsibilities to the government, an idea not found anywhere in the New Testament).

The gifts of the Spirit are meant to be used, not ignored. Your place in the organization can't be easily duplicated by someone

---

* Commonly called the 80/20 rule, where 20% of the people perform 80% of the work. Sadly in some churches it's more like 90/10 or 95/5.

else as you're uniquely qualified to perform that role. If you're not doing what you're equipped to do you're denying the church something God wants us to have, reducing the military effectiveness of your larger unit.

Yet too often spiritual gifts become a point of contention, a condition resulting from a failure to understand their role, and the military organization of the church. Let's return to the Marines once again. How effective would the Fire Team unit be if the machine gunner always complained about not having the grenade launcher? Pathetic, right?

The church does argue over who gets which gifts, with results just as pathetic. Have you ever been in a church that argues over who gets to do what? It's sad because it's God who places each person in their role, so if we're arguing over who gets to carry the machine gun, we're saying God doesn't know what He's doing. That, of course, is pride, a problem getting a certain angel into a bit of trouble.

CHAPTER XXI

Why Do We Fail?

ARE YOU READY TO BEGIN YOUR JOURNEY toward a spiritually combat-ready, well-equipped Christian? Good. Like any skill, you can't just jump in at the end, you need background in the fundamentals: in order to fix the problem, you must *understand* the problem. We've already identified two problems:

- Compartmentalizing life. It's *all* God's box.
- Failure to be honest about our ability and training.

It's that second issue we'll spend much time on. Why do we fail, and why are too many Christians not combat-ready? Surprisingly, the answer breaks down to four simple areas. If you don't believe Satan and his cohorts exist, they're out to fight you and bring you down, and to effectively mount a military campaign requires your knowledge, training, and dedication then put this down right now and go watch re-runs of "I Love Lucy." Seriously.

Knowledge

We don't study the Word of God, and you can't apply what you don't know. Many Christians can't perform the most basic skills — sure, they're great at pot-lucks, but that's not a skill helping you in a spiritual dark alley at 3 AM. If they enter into combat in that condition, well, you *do* remember what happens to the pig, don't you?

If you enter battle thinking you're prepared, and you meet an adversary who *is* prepared, how ugly do you think the outcome will be? Do you think you stand a chance?

The reason we lack knowledge remains simple — too many pastors sermonize or preach, instead of teaching the Word of God line by line, verse by verse, through the *entire* Bible. As we'll discuss later (but should be obvious anyway), a soldier never enters combat with part of his gear. Moreover, he carefully examines it to be sure it's all in working order.

Do you have an area of the Bible you're not exactly familiar with? It's time to dig in. If you're in a church where the pastor fails to teach the complete Bible (verse by verse, chapter by chapter, book by book), you might want to consider your situation and see if that's an environment getting you in shape.

With the advent of the Internet you have the opportunity to acquire personal tutoring by some of the best teachers. If you haven't listened to Chuck Smith's teaching on the entire Bible that's a good place to start (if you ever hope to advance). You can acquire Chuck's complete teaching on the Bible from The Word for Today on MP3 for about $30. If you're serious about your training, you *must* begin at the beginning. You'll never advance without the basic foundation, and Chuck's studies provide the best foundation you can get. Period. No question. Without a doubt.

Training

Knowledge by itself isn't worth much. You could possess the knowledge of a sixth-degree black belt, but if you haven't trained the knowledge is useless; a huge difference exists between spectator and participant. Remember, our goal is the ability to *function* as a black belt, not simply look cool spouting the lingo.

And for that, you'll require training. Lots of it. And then more. Over many years. Most people are familiar with Paul's list of the armor of God in Ephesians 6. You might not know the Roman army innovated a revolutionary sword radically different from all others, giving the soldier a tactical advantage to win combat at close range using superior equipment and tactics.

Only one problem with it — it required years of training, drill, and practice to master its advantages. If you were just handed one and sent to battle (even if you knew it was the best weapon available) you would be butchered (like a pig ... again); knowledge and equipment by itself isn't sufficient.

The Christian has available the most advanced spiritual weapons in existence, yet faces the same situation the Roman soldier did with their sword — to be able to use the equipment to gain an advantage requires training. Lots of it.

Let's be honest — training is *boring*, which is why not many do it. Many Taekwondo students drop out because going from white belt to black belt requires effort and work. Yet if you hope to win, you must train. The average Christian sits warming a pew week after month, but never trains on their own, and that's a recipe (no, a guarantee) for failure.

Dedication and Perseverance

Even if you're trained, if you quit easily you're toast. You can acquire the best knowledge, be trained by the best instructor, but if you don't persist when the going gets tough, you'll never make it. Sadly, we've raised a lazy generation of people who can't think, and believe everyone possesses an innate entitlement to certain things — even if that requires forceful removal from someone else. Whatever happened to winning through hard work?

In today's politically correct world, perhaps you've seen young kids baseball (or other sports) where nobody keeps score, and everyone gets a trophy. That's a load of horse manure, to be polite*. As John Loeffler says, we've gone from being right to feeling good about being wrong. Lacking dedication and perseverance, you won't make it. That's certainly contrary to everybody's-a-winner namby-pamby philosophy, but it's reality. Never quit, never give in, never surrender.

Preparedness

You need equipment in good working order, and you need that *before* the battle. Any equipment must be constantly prepared and ready for battle, as once you need it it's too late. That's obvious to be sure, but how many people haven't done basic Bible memory work? Oh, that's for kids' Sunday School, you say, to get gold stars.

Negative. It's for *you*, and becomes part of your preparedness. Sadly, Bible memory has fallen out of style, but you should easily be able to imagine a situation where you need your Bible, but for some reason don't have one. In that case, the only thing you've got is what you've got — what you've memorized. Failing

---

* We're not talking about being uncivilized or poor sports, but the fact remains somebody wins, and somebody loses.

Bible memory, you're unprepared, and we're back to being the pig again.

Second, you must always live in "condition yellow." Simply put, that means *always* be prepared for conflict, as it can come anytime. No, we're not talking about a paranoid devil-behind-every-corner delusion, but a realistic approach meaning trouble can come at any place, any time. If you hope to increase your effectiveness, you've got to have an honest appraisal about reality, you need to be well trained, and you need to be prepared *always*.

Unless you want to be the pig.

CHAPTER XXII

Get in the Game

WE'VE COME TO WHERE THE RUBBER MEETS the road. We've uncovered Zechariah and Haggai's lessons, and you must realize by now we're in the same situation. You've seen the problem, understood reality, and so on. Now we come to the plan, it's time to put the Bon-Bons down, get off the couch, and get in the game!

Where are you? It's not a question of how long you've been a Christian, it's a question of how long you've been training. As Yoda would say "do or do not, there is no try." This requires a lifestyle change, not a quick-fix program for what ails you. It's not snake oil.

The challenge is: do you *want* to? If you don't want to, put the book down and go back to watching "Laverne and Shirley" re-runs. If you're ready (and by now you should be), let's "gird up our loins" as the King James says (meaning be prepared for action), and get to the plan. Your training program begins *now*. We're going to throw the kitchen sink at you in this final section, covering *lots* of ground.

It's 2:59 AM

You're almost out of time ... will you be ready?

At 3 AM you've got what you've got, nobody to lean on, nobody to call. It's just you and whatever crisis lies on the other end of the phone. Will you be prepared to pick it up?

Perhaps Job provides the prototype for the 3 AM phone call. Here he was, minding his own business (and living a righteous life, as it turns out), and blammo! His world crumbles around him in a few minutes. Job of course, didn't have the advantage we do — that of chapter 1. All he knew was suddenly his world turned upside down.

His wife wasn't much help (whose wonderful advice was "curse God and die"), and when his "friends" show up, they're not much help either. Through thirty chapters or so we're treated to much useless conversation as Job's friends try to get to the root of the problem, but can't.

Perhaps you find yourself in a similar situation. Maybe you've had friends say the answer to why the innocent suffer comes from the book of Job. There's only one problem with that — it's totally false. You see, if Job's book should answer the question of why the innocent suffer, nothing answers that question. No, the real point of the book comes about chapter 38.

> *Then the Lord answered Job out of the whirlwind, and said, Who is this that darkeneth counsel by words without knowledge? Gird up now thy loins like a man; for I will demand of thee, and answer thou me. Where wast thou when I laid the foundations of the earth?* Job 38:1-4

Job's book provides the divine viewpoint — or as Bill Ritchie says "if God is God, then God is God," meaning simply He's God, and you're not, so don't expect to understand everything that transpires. Job certainly didn't. When you can go through trials and the first thought is trying to get the divine viewpoint, you're on your way.

It's not easy, it's work, but it's 2:59 AM and the clock continues to tick — will you be ready when the clock strikes 3 AM?

What Happens At 3 AM?

So what happens at 3 AM? This is where the rubber meets the road. Two people go to the doctor with tumors but receive a different diagnosis. For one, it's benign, for the other, it's inoperable (and terminal).

Both families prayed. Where is God? Why didn't He hear our requests? You see, God is not a genie granting wishes. If you've studied Job, you know it's vital to get the divine viewpoint. For the first family, they're praising God, thank you for hearing! The second family, not so much.

But wait ... did God change? Did His mercy, love, and goodness suddenly not become available to the person who wasn't healed? Of course not. While those two people will have much different reactions, it's important to know God hasn't changed ... only our perception of Him.

And *that's* the divine viewpoint. Nobody said it was easy.

Zig Ziglar remains a popular motivational speaker. I heard him once say growing up in Yazoo City, the most exciting thing to happen was when the train would come trough town. But when he explained they didn't have any train tracks in town it made the story more interesting!*

Zig tells a story about his many travels; he flew a lot. Zig relates (and I'll paraphrase) he got so when waiting in line (back when you could deal with a person), he could tell when a new position was about to open up. Being tired from his trip, he wanted to be first in line, so he waited, ready to pounce.

Well, the person behind the counter took down the "position closed" sign, and put up the "position open" sign, and Zig was ready, he was first as the lady behind the counter told him the 3 o'clock flight he was on had been canceled. Bummer.

Zig replied "fantastic" (seriously, not sarcastically — I told you Zig was a bit different) as the lady continued to tell him he would be delayed for several hours, to which Zig again replied "fantastic." Now the lady is puzzled, she just *had* to ask, sir, I just told you your flight was canceled, and you've now got a long layover before you can get home, how can you say fantastic? Zig replied, ma'am, there's only three reasons why anyone would cancel my flight.

1. Something must be wrong with that airplane.
2. Something must be wrong with the guy who's going to fly that airplane.
3. Something must be wrong with the weather he's going to fly that airplane in.

And ma'am, if *any* of those conditions exist, I don't want to be up there, I want to be right down here, so I say fantastic. Well, Zig certainly has a unique way to look at life.

All that is prologue to the point. Zig has a way of hammering the point your attitude relates to your overall outlook. So back to the doctor. Suppose you visit the doctor for an illness, and he prescribes some medicine to cure the condition. Naturally, you must return after a period of time for a checkup. The doctor flips though your chart, studies the results, and comes to one of several conclusions.

---

*   Zig's book "See you at the Top" is highly recommended

- Your body is *reacting* to the medicine.
- Your body is *responding* to the medicine.

Do you notice the difference between the two? The question is: do you respond or react to situations? You can't control what happens to you, but you can control your response, a response affecting people around you, your family, your friends.

Will you respond or react at 3 AM? The choice is yours, but note in order to have the correct response, you must decide beforehand how you'll handle it, and you must be prepared. Unprepared people don't fare well, but those who previously determine a course of action come through much better.

Remember Daniel? In chapter 1, we see Daniel decide *before* any later events that he would not defile himself. When we see him later, his steadfastness wasn't something he came up with on the spot, he predetermined how he would handle the situation.

One problem stems from the popular myth we'll rise to the occasion when crisis comes. Usually that's not true. You won't rise to the occasion, you'll fall to the level of your training, thus it's critical to your Christian life to be prepared *before* crunch time arrives.

Step one on your journey forward remains simple: determine now how you'll prepare yourself for the trials you know will be coming. Everyone has trials, some come through them, some stumble over them, and some crumble in them. The common characteristic of those who come out the other side will be they prepared *before* the crisis began.

Because at 3 AM, you've got what you've got.

Verse by Verse Bible Study

If you're not in a church teaching verse by verse through the entire Bible, you probably should find a new church. Harsh? Perhaps. But sermonizing over a favorite topic, or preaching on church pot lucks, or good works won't help your training. Only a systematic study of the entire Bible will get the job done.

Sadly, many "pastors" don't understand this. If yours doesn't, try and politely tell him he's not adequately preparing you for what lies ahead, and ask him to pick a book and teach through it verse by verse. Hopefully, you'll have a new well-equipped pastor. If he rejects your idea, you'll have a tough choice to make.

There's simply no substitute for a systematic study of the entire Bible — it's the only way you can grasp the entirety of

God's plan, and avoid focusing only on whatever someone finds to be their favorite section or idea.

How can you begin? You can obtain Chuck Smith's entire Bible commentary on MP3 for about $30. It's the best $30 you'll spend. Get an MP3 player, load 'em up, and start traveling through the Bible.

You'll Get Dinged

If you've trained in marital arts or almost any other sport, you quickly realize sometimes you'll get hurt in training. That's just the way it is. Don't let that distract you, as injuries you might get during training are usually less than what you'll get in actual combat. You must learn how to work through adversity (read the epilogue for what happened while writing this book).

> *No man that warreth entangleth himself with the affairs of this life; that he may please him who hath chosen him to be a soldier.*
> 2 Timothy 2:4

CHAPTER XXIII

Strategy

OKAY, YOU'VE GOT A PLAN SO LET'S HANDLE some common issues and basic strategy. These issues may not appear to be related to your journey, but be guaranteed sooner or later you will encounter them, and not many pastors cover them. We're going to cover considerable ground in this chapter so please return your seat to the upright position and close your tray table.

23.1 The Scientific Method

WHILE NOT A MAJOR TOPIC IN logic or philosophy classes, failure to understand (and use) the scientific method causes problems in logic, critical thinking, and even theology, ultimately denying foundational characteristics of God.

Scientific Method Defined

A method of research in which a problem is identified, relevant data gathered, a hypothesis formulated from data, and the hypothesis empirically tested. A rather obvious idea — examine data and reality and determine if it matches what you predict or expect, then update your ideas to match results; while steps may be added, the scientific method boils down to a few simple principals:

1. Make a guess (idea)
2. Test it (collect data, experiment, etc.)
3. Modify idea based on results (reality)
4. Lather, rinse, repeat

Not difficult, and it's hard to imagine disputing the common sense of it. After all, only members of the tin-foil-hat brigade fail to update ideas based on reality.

Sadly, that's *exactly* what some do, clutching bizarre delusional ideas in spite of reality (i.e. flat-earthers, etc.). As John Loeffler says, eventually reality becomes reality, and delusional ideas represent the precise opposite of the scientific method.

However, step one often throws people off. Science does *not* require step one to be correct. Any wild guess begins the process; matching with experiment counts, and if not, modifying the original idea until it does.

Christians often become anti-science due to one person: Darwin. Darwin wasn't Satan, he noticed something he couldn't explain, created a theory (guess, hypothesis) to explain it, and stated predictions which would support his idea if true (i.e. innumerable fossilized transitional forms should be found).

Later data doesn't support his theory, and evolution (biology) remains a field not following the scientific method. It matters not how brilliant an idea appears to be, if it doesn't match with reality (data, experiment), it's wrong.

> *The principle of science, the definition, almost, is the following: The test of all knowledge is experiment. Experiment is the sole judge of scientific "truth"** ~ Richard Feynman

Why Does It Work?

The scientific method works for *one* reason — the God of the universe created it and created order and consistent rules for the universe to follow. When you drop an apple, nobody ponders the direction it will travel, it drops to the ground. Always.

Why? God is a god of order. Reason. Logic. The scientific method, properly used, provides a method to discover *how* God designed the universe and the principals governing its existence.

Biblical Examples

For those believing religion is (or should be) anti-science, God Himself provides examples of the scientific method. Man didn't invent the scientific method, he only discovered what God created.

Daniel

> *Daniel spoke with the attendant who had been appointed by the chief of staff to look after Daniel, Hananiah, Mishael, and*

---

* "The Feynman Lectures on Physics", Volume I page 1-1

> *Azariah.* "*Please test us for ten days on a diet of vegetables and water,*" *Daniel said.* "*At the end of the ten days, see how we look compared to the other young men who are eating the king's food. Then make your decision in light of what you see.*"
>
> *The attendant agreed to Daniel's suggestion and tested them for ten days. At the end of the ten days, Daniel and his three friends looked healthier and better nourished than the young men who had been eating the food assigned by the king.*
>
> Daniel 1:11-15 NLT

As a kosher Jew, Daniel didn't want to eat non-kosher food, even if the best the King could offer. Instead he proposed an idea — let's follow the scientific method and test what happens if we eat only kosher food, not the King's menu.

1. Make a guess — we'll be in better shape if we stay kosher and eat only vegetables.
2. Experiment — feed us for 10 days and see what happens.
3. Modify based on results — after 10 days, they were in better shape; the attendant thereafter fed them only vegetables.

A perfect example of the scientific method, used by one of the pillars of the Bible. Never forget, Paul reminds us in Romans 15:4 what was written before was for *our* learning, so people ignoring the scientific method not only contradict God, but ignore Paul's teaching as well.

God Himself Uses The Method

In Malachi, the Lord lays out problems of His people. They respond "we didn't do that, how did we do that?" And the Lord provides the proof.

One area involved the tithe, or giving 10%. For our purposes, don't become distracted whether this applies today or not, or if poor people should tithe, or anything else (we're focused on science, not the religious aspect).

> "*Bring all the tithes into the storehouse so there will be enough food in my Temple. If you do,*" *says the Lord of Heaven's Armies,* "*I will open the windows of heaven for you. I will pour out a blessing so great you won't have enough room to take it in! Try it! Put me to the test!*"
>
> Malachi 3:10 NLT

What does the Lord do? Propose a test — try Me and see (perform an experiment and examine the results). When the creator of the universe validates an idea, it's something we should listen to; those rejecting the scientific method reject God's nature, and thus, God Himself.

One branch of science denies the scientific method. Evolution (recall Piltdown man?). A question to the reader — do you (or your pastor) want to align with the foolishness of evolution? Evolution has *no* experimental evidence for its foundations:

1. First there was nothing (matter comes from nothing).
2. And then it exploded (explosions produce order).
3. From the goo to the zoo (abiogenesis — life comes from non-life).
4. To you (new species evolve from mutations).

If you don't have all four, evolution doesn't work. Period. Yet where are peer-reviewed reproducible scientific experiments for those four items? Lacking that, evolution is un-scientific *by definition.*

In contrast, the Bible and God demonstrate the scientific method. God gave you a brain, and provided examples on how to use it.

The scientific method works.

People in the Bible used it.

God Himself validates it.

That should be enough.

Don't be Anti-Science

The dawn of the pandemic era (2020–2021) saw many pastors willfully reject God as they rejected science. They probably didn't stand in the pulpit on Sunday and proclaim they're rebelling against God, but by denying science they reject God, whether they admit it or not. As the pandemic raged, pastors and others made foolish statements like:

- It's only a few cases, it won't affect us here.
- It's no worse than flu.*
- We don't need to filter the air, create distance, sanitize, or take any precautions.

---

* Final data will take years to analyze, but covid turned out to considerably worse than "just the flu," no matter the metric used (deaths, number of infections, length of illness, severity of symptoms, etc.)

All those are wrong, as the scientific method (and reality) proves. The data exists for them, and sadly many "Christians" willfully rebelled against God and His designed order to deny reality, science, and common sense at the dawn of the pandemic age. Don't be anti-science — anti-science is anti-God.

The scientific method, properly used, might be God's greatest natural gift to us. Follow God's example, when you have an idea, create an experiment (or look at actual data) and then *modify your idea based on results (reality)*.

The last part remains key. Don't be stubborn and cling to ideas data and reality prove incorrect. Yes, it's difficult to be humble and admit you're wrong, but everyone makes mistakes; it's silly (and stupid) firmly clutching ideas reality proves completely incorrect.

Do Your Homework

As Chuck Missler says, don't believe anything I (or anyone else) told you — you're called to be a skeptic (Acts 17:11). Do your own work and use logic, thinking skills, and methods God provided you. If you blindly accept ideas without checking them out for yourself you've failed the course. Follow the scientific method, it's one of the best tools God provided us.

23.2 Trust the Math

IF YOU'VE BEEN A CHRISTIAN for a long time, you've likely encountered someone asking a question similar to "can you provide a few verses on salvation," or eternal security, or where you go when you die, or something else.

Why are those difficult questions to answer? In math, if a student must review the quadratic formula it's trivial to locate the section explaining it. Not so with the Bible; it's unique by design (and intention), which explains why those questions persist.

The Bible must hold one quality math books need not concern themselves with — the intent of attack by enemies to jam and prevent its message from going forth. Nobody dissects an algebra text and rips out sections on quadratic formulas. Yet many desire to rip-out sections of the Bible:

- Peter didn't author that book, so don't consider what he wrote as authoritative.
- Modern translations using the "critical" text (i.e. Westcott and Hort's magic deletions).

- Daniel was written later by a forger, after the so-called "prophecy" of events.

Scholars debate and discuss (perhaps voting) on what Jesus said, which books of the Bible are written by the author, and when it was written. Ridiculous theories like the documentary hypothesis (Moses didn't write the books bearing his name), the equally laughable deutero-Isaiah theory, Daniel didn't write when he did (but his book appears in the Septuagint so no matter the page count on their thesis, it can't post-date the Septuagint).

Scholars attack the *entire* Bible, as God anticipated pseudo-scholarship and the bogus theories it spawns. Thus, no single chapter in the Bible exists as the "salvation" chapter; the message spreads across the entire book, as revealed in Isaiah.

But the word of the LORD was unto them precept upon precept, precept upon precept; line upon line, line upon line; here a little, and there a little;   Isaiah 28:13

To understand doctrine, the complete Bible must be studied as an integrated system, not picking and choosing favorite parts.

On the spectrum's other end of the science-deniers rest the feeling people, reducing Christianity to feelings and opinion. I *think* Jesus wouldn't have done xyz, therefore if He *did* speak on it, the Bible must be wrong and we should (must) ignore that section. An example from Isaiah 14:12–15 shows the error of believing your opinion overrules God — it didn't work out well for the guy trying it.

If you've ever had the opportunity to watch an illusionist live and in-person, you can stare directly at him, and you *know* he didn't saw the person in half, yet that's what you observed and witnessed. Will you believe your lying eyes? Or logical thinking skills?

Peter states an idea you might think strange at first, but in light of the previous makes 100% sense.

For we have not followed cunningly devised fables, when we made known unto you the power and coming of our Lord Jesus Christ, but were eyewitnesses of his majesty. For he received from God the Father honor and glory, when there came such a voice to him from the excellent glory, This is my beloved Son, in whom I am well pleased.   2 Peter 1:16–17

Peter was *there* for most of Jesus' events, yet he tackles this vital subject and it's important because it applies to *us*, not just those who watched Jesus two thousand years ago, as he continues with a strange idea.

> *We have also a more sure word of prophecy; whereunto ye do well that ye take heed, as unto a light that shineth in a dark place, until the day dawn, and the day star arise in your hearts*

Peter states he was *there* for the events of Jesus' life, yet don't believe his eyewitness account, look to the more sure word of prophecy, and tosses in the additional thought if you want to be a smart person, you would do well to heed prophecy over what he saw — if you want to be smart in Peter's sense, don't believe gossip, unsubstantiated conspiracies, political nonsense, misquotes, or even your eyes.

Without diverting into a detailed analysis (others have), considering all the prophecies of Jesus and making guesses as to the probability of each (i.e. what are the odds of a person being born in Bethlehem?), obtaining a composite probability and considering the result, it's mathematically *impossible* for Jesus not to be who He said He was when viewed through a prophetic lens.

The probability numbers become more than the number of atoms in the universe, as if you marked a single atom somewhere in the universe, and you must pick the correct one on the first try. It rounds to zero — which explains why critics try to late-date Daniel and others for example, they know math proves prophecy and the Bible.

Trust. The. Math.

In the end, almost everything reduces to math. Economics, politics, pandemics, science, biology, and knowing the Bible all boil down to math.

The Bible demonstrates logical principles, which often are misunderstood (and misused).

> *If there arise among you a prophet, or a dreamer of dreams, and giveth thee a sign or a wonder, And the sign or the wonder come to pass, whereof he spoke unto thee, saying, Let us go after other gods, which thou hast not known, and let us serve them; Thou shalt not hearken unto the words of that prophet, or that dreamer of dreams: for the LORD your God proveth you, to know whether ye love the LORD your God with all your heart and with all your soul.* Deuteronomy 13:1–3

Even *if* a "prophet" arises, performs miracles or predicts the future, but contradicts God's Word, he remains a false prophet. Don't believe your eyes, believe God's Word.

Another fashionable trend remains "updating the Bible for modern times" — a bad idea as God remains constant, yet many state portions of God's Word don't apply today, or the scientific rules governing the cosmos since its creation don't apply either.

Principle #1 — Miracles do NOT Validate a Prophet

The magicians in Egypt duplicated Moses' miracles ... up to a point. Pharaoh failed to understand miracles can't be used to validate a true prophet of God. Deuteronomy 18 repeats a similar warning, but from a different perspective.

> *But the prophet, which shall presume to speak a word in my name, which I have not commanded him to speak, or that shall speak in the name of other gods, even that prophet shall die. And if thou say in thine heart, How shall we know the word which the LORD hath not spoken? When a prophet speaketh in the name of the LORD, if the thing follow not, nor come to pass, that is the thing which the LORD hath not spoken, but the prophet hath spoken it presumptuously: thou shalt not be afraid of him.*   Deuteronomy 18:20–22

Here's where math comes in — Deuteronomy 13 proclaims a false prophet can perform miracles (which we know from Egypt) so DO NOT use that to validate; Deuteronomy 18 sets the standard for God's prophets as 100% accuracy — if a claimed prophet's events do not come to pass, he's not a prophet from God.

Principle #2 — Failure of prophecy Means a False Prophet

In math terms the Converse of a statement is not necessarily true. It *may* be, but you don't know it and it must be proved apart from the original idea.

- If A, then B
- Converse: If B, then A
- Inverse: If Not A, then not B
- Contrapositive: If not B, then not A

From the original statement, only the last can be assumed as true. The contrapositive of Deuteronomy 18 obtains the statement often repeated in Christian circles: A true prophet of God states prophecies which *always* come true with 100% accuracy. It's logically equivalent to Deuteronomy 18.

A simpler example might provide clarity. Suppose we say "If I am on the couch, then I am in my house" we can logically form the following statements:

- If I am in the house, then I am on the couch.
- If I am not on the couch, I am not in the house.
- Contrapositive: If I am not in my house, I am not on the couch.

It's obvious the converse and inverse may — or may not — be true, as a person could be in the kitchen, for example, or be sitting on the couch.

Back to Peter. Peter says you would do well to heed math and logical analysis; don't be anti-science, anti-logic, or anti-math — those positions contradict the Bible's teaching. Peter provides the answer to a frequent and troubling question — why send a prophet when they won't heed the message?

> *And he said unto me, Son of man, I send thee to the children of Israel, to a rebellious nation that hath rebelled against me: they and their fathers have transgressed against me, even unto this very day. For they are impudent children and stiff-hearted. I do send thee unto them; and thou shalt say unto them, Thus saith the Lord GOD. And they, whether they will hear, or whether they will forbear, (for they are a rebellious house,) yet shall know that there hath been a prophet among them.* Ezekiel 2:3–5

Sure, people are rebellious and not many listen, but then they are without excuse when they *know* a prophet and God's message has been among them. Certainly true, but a more troubling question remains, why send the prophet when the Lord knows *nobody* will listen, as God tells Jeremiah.

> *Since the day that your fathers came forth out of the land of Egypt unto this day I have even sent unto you all my servants the prophets, daily rising up early and sending them: Yet they hearkened not unto me, nor inclined their ear, but hardened their neck: they did worse than their fathers. Therefore thou shalt speak all these words unto them; but they will not hearken to thee: thou shalt also call unto them; but they will not answer thee.* Jeremiah 7:25–27

Two reasons for sending prophets to stiff-necked rebellious people:

1. So *they* know a prophet has been among them.
2. As Peter says, so *we* validate the math.

Jeremiah writes more than many prophets, and he's one the Lord told the people won't accept the message; a reason besides the obvious of warning the people of Jeremiah's day *must* be involved, and Peter reveals it. We wouldn't have the message if the Lord told Jeremiah "don't bother with them, they won't listen" — we need Jeremiah's writing as Peter says trust the math of the prophets. Daniel *lived* Peter's words:

> *In the first year of his reign I Daniel understood by books the number of the years, whereof the word of the LORD came to Jeremiah the prophet, that he would accomplish seventy years in the desolations of Jerusalem.* Daniel 9

Daniel acknowledges two things: Jeremiah was a prophet, and he takes what Jeremiah said literally — 70 years are almost up. Notice no chapter exists on *trust the math*, but it's everywhere (here a little, there a little), and math's logical rules are explicit in the Bible.

Daniel foreshadowed what Peter would say much later: trust the math, and take prophecy literally. Daniel also lived Peter's next thought.

> *Knowing this first, that no prophecy of the scripture is of any private interpretation. For the prophecy came not in old time by the will of man: but holy men of God spoke as they were moved by the Holy Ghost.* 2 Peter 1

It's not private, but out in the open. Logical rules are available to anyone who *wants* to learn. Sadly, some don't, but it's not because it's secret or unavailable. Daniel didn't read Jeremiah and wonder, what does 70 years mean?

> *But there were false prophets also among the people, even as there shall be false teachers among you, who secretly shall bring in damnable heresies, even denying the Lord that bought them, and bring upon themselves swift destruction. And many shall follow their pernicious ways; by reason of whom the way of truth shall be evil spoken of.* 2 Peter 2:1–2

Victims are those who don't trust math, and many follow them. Commonly called tin-foil hat people, flat-earth, science deniers, and those in similar states of denial.

If people abandon logic, thinking, and science they'll wander — slowly at first — and end up far from the truth (read that: far from God and the Bible). False teachers *will* exist in the church. One way to uncover them is they don't trust the math — they can be anti-science, anti-math, anti-logic, fail to modify their position when new evidence appears, fight and screech for their opinion, and become hostile to anyone who questions their idea or dares ask for evidence.

Questions are *always* acceptable on *any* subject as truth can withstand scrutiny (it's fine to discuss flat-earth theory, but it will be a short conversation). Those becoming hostile when legitimate questions come up (or fail to modify their position when evidence demands) provide a clue they don't have reality backing up their opinion.

Trust the math.

At 3 AM or any other time.

23.3 Seventy Weeks of Daniel

THE FAMOUS 70 WEEKS OF Daniel. Even people knowing nothing else of the book have heard of this passage. It's vital to understand this section before you arrive at Revelation or you'll be completely lost; Matthew underscores the importance of the prophecy as it's *specifically* called out for understanding.

> *When ye therefore shall see the abomination of desolation, spoken of by Daniel the prophet, stand in the holy place,* **(whoso readeth, let him understand)**　　　　　　　　　　Matt 24:15

Consider the verses in context, as they form the framework to understand all prophecy.

> *Seventy weeks are determined upon thy people and upon thy holy city, to finish the transgression, and to make an end of sins, and to make reconciliation for iniquity, and to bring in everlasting righteousness, and to seal up the vision and prophecy, and to anoint the most Holy.*
>
> *Know therefore and understand, that from the going forth of the commandment to restore and to build Jerusalem unto the Messiah the Prince shall be seven weeks, and threescore and*

> *two weeks; the street shall be built again, and the wall, even in troublous times.*
>
> *And after threescore and two weeks shall Messiah be cut off, but not for himself; and the people of the prince that shall come shall destroy the city and the sanctuary; and the end thereof shall be with a flood, and unto the end of the war desolations are determined. And he shall confirm the covenant with many for one week; and in the midst of the week he shall cause the sacrifice and the oblation to cease, and for the overspreading of abominations he shall make it desolate, even until the consummation, and that determined shall be poured upon the desolate.*
> Daniel 9:24–27

Note the implicit technology — when you see. We immediately take that for granted, but prior to satellite TV and Internet, only a few could see the Holy Place at once, while these events will be viewable worldwide. It's only recently (since the 1970s or so) where technology existed for the world to watch events unfold live.

A few notes to avoid bad information, and should be obvious from even a casual reading (though surprisingly many miss):

- It's about the Jews, *not* the church. It's Daniel's people (the Jews) and their Holy City (Jerusalem).
- It hasn't happened yet. The end of sin, everlasting righteousness, and so on. Some attempt to claim a previous fulfillment, but then the news must have skipped reporting the end of sin and the beginning of everlasting righteousness.
- The seventy weeks are not continuous. A gap appears between the 69th week and the 70th week.
- Revelation details the 70th week (mainly chapters 6–19).

Keeping a few facts in mind avoids pitfalls and places you ahead of scholars who don't read the book. You'll notice God deals with the church and Jews separately. Before Jesus, God dealt with the Jews (Gentiles were only included if they became a Jew). Since Jesus' death and resurrection, God dealt with the Gentiles. This leads some to believe God abandoned the Jews, and their promises are now bestowed on the church.

Nonsense — God's promises to Abraham in Genesis are unconditional and irrevocable; the Jewish people still have a destiny to be fulfilled. Don't believe the Jews aren't important anymore, or God's promises to them have now fallen on the church.

We'll break the prophecy down into a few sections:

- v24 — Overview.
- v25 — The sixty-nine weeks (complete).
- v26a — The Messiah.
- v26b — The interval between week sixty-nine and seventy (where we're currently at).
- v27 — The final week (still future, but detailed in Revelation).

The Overview

Seventy weeks are determined upon thy people and upon thy holy city, to finish the transgression, and to make an end of sins, and to make reconciliation for iniquity, and to bring in everlasting righteousness, and to seal up the vision and prophecy, and to anoint the most Holy. Daniel 9:24

As noted, it's obvious this prophecy concerns the Jews and the city of Jerusalem, not the Church. Second, while history records the fulfillment of parts of the prophecy, parts remain future. Obviously, an end of sin hasn't occurred, nor everlasting righteousness.

What are the seventy weeks? The Hebrew says seventy sevens, and it's translated weeks. Similar to our use of decade (meaning ten years), in this context the Hebrew clearly implies a week means seven years. One note; Bible prophecy uses 360 day years. Why isn't important, but if calculating this yourself you can't use the current 365-day calendar.

It does represent a literal period — it's not an allegory and must be understood to be literal. To jump ahead a bit, several allusions to the 70th week appear elsewhere in the Bible, each describing the time a bit differently, yet equally.

- 42 months — Revelation 11:2, 13:5
- 1,260 days — Revelation 11:3, 12:6
- Half of one week (literally "sevens") — Daniel 9:27
- Times, time and half a time (3 ½ years) — Daniel 12:7

Notice 1260 divided by 3.5 = 360 — a year in the Bible equals 360 days. Chuck Missler notes ancient calendars changed around 700 BC from 360 days to the current 365 ¼ days, although each did differently. Why the change occurred might be historically interesting, but not important here, and left as an exercise for the interested reader.

The 69 Weeks

> *Know therefore and understand, that from the going forth of the commandment to restore and to build Jerusalem unto the Messiah the Prince shall be seven weeks, and threescore and two weeks; the street shall be built again, and the wall, even in troublous times.*
> Daniel 9:25

For most of this discussion, we're going to use Sir Robert Anderson's work "The Coming Prince," cited by Chuck Missler, J Vernon McGee, and most other scholars (no we didn't do all this work ourselves).

Notice it's a prediction, with a starting event, mathematical number, and a terminating event. This should be easy to verify or disprove for critics. It's the exact nature of this prophecy (and others in Daniel) leading skeptics to late date the book by a pen other than Daniel's. The research exists on shaky ground, but the presumption is God doesn't exist, therefore prophecy doesn't exist, thus it's impossible for Daniel to have known the future with such precision.

Daniel's error is zero. Compare to the prophets you'll find in the National Enquirer (or political or economic pundits) who receive great accolades if they get it *half* right. Bible prophets maintain 100% accuracy, and would be stoned if something uttered failed to come true — the yardstick for prophets of God is 100% accuracy, all the time.

> *But the prophet, which shall presume to speak a word in my name, which I have not commanded him to speak, or that shall speak in the name of other gods, even that prophet shall die. And if thou say in thine heart, How shall we know the word which the LORD hath not spoken? When a prophet speaketh in the name of the LORD, if the thing follow not, nor come to pass, that is the thing which the LORD hath not spoken, but the prophet hath spoken it presumptuously; thou shalt not be afraid of him.*
> Deuteronomy 18:20–22

Let's break down the sixty-nine weeks for further analysis:

- START: from the going forth of the command to restore and build Jerusalem.
- NUMBER: There shall be seven weeks and sixty-two weeks.
- FINAL EVENT: Until Messiah the Prince.

When did this start? Perhaps your Bible mentions three possibilities for this event (actually four).

- Cyrus in Ezra 1:1-4 (First year of Cyrus)
- Darius in Ezra 6:1-12 (First year of Darius)
- Artaxerxes in Ezra 7:11-26 (Seventh year Artaxerxes)
- Artaxerxes in Nehemiah 2:1-8 (Twentieth year Artaxerxes)

So which is it? Return to the text to discover one more clue "The street shall be built again, and the wall, even in troublous times." Only Nehemiah mentions the wall, with the decree occurring in 445 BC in the month of Nisan. Notice how simple Bible prophecy becomes when you just take what it says as what it means? Imagine all the problems we'd have if we tried to allegorize it. Accept it as it says and you'll be fine.

Mark Eastman in his book "The Search for Messiah" states it's Hebrew tradition when the day of month isn't mentioned specifically it means the first day*. According to Nehemiah, the starting point is the first of Nisan in the twentieth year of Artaxerxes. The interval is easy as 69 weeks of 360 day years is 173,880 days. What's the final event? Until the coming of the Jewish Messiah. And that's the whole prophecy.

If you do the calendar work, moving forward from Nisan 445 BC 173,880 days you'll arrive at the tenth of Nisan 32 AD [†], known as April 6, 32 AD. So What? The significance comes from Jesus himself, after the events of what we call Palm Sunday, as He weeps over the city.

> *And when he was come near, he beheld the city, and wept over it, Saying, If thou hadst known, even thou, at least in this thy day, the things which belong unto thy peace! But now they are hid from thine eyes. For the days shall come upon thee, that thine enemies shall cast a trench about thee, and compass thee round, and keep thee in on every side, And shall lay thee even with the ground, and thy children within thee; and they shall not leave in thee one stone upon another; because thou knewest not the time of thy visitation.* Luke 19:41-44

As you read the Gospels, you'll notice a few times the crowd tries to make Him king, but He slips away, saying My time has

---

* http://blueletterbible.org/Comm/mark_eastman/messiah/sfm_06.html
† McGee (1982, page 588)

not yet come. On this specific day, He not only allowed it, He arranged it. Why? It's the exact day from the prophecy in Daniel.

Jesus held them accountable to know. The prophecy isn't hard to understand, and if we can figure out the events thousands of years later, the Jews certainly should have understood. It's not allegorical or theoretical; the creator of the universe holds people accountable to what He's said. Something else must explain why the Jews missed it.

> *The scepter shall not depart from Judah, nor a lawgiver from between his feet, until Shiloh come; and unto him shall the gathering of the people be.* Genesis 49:10

To distill the verse, it means the Jews would not have capital punishment taken away from them until the Messiah appears. As Rome takes over Israel, the Jewish leaders lament, for they think the scripture has been broken. Yet they did not know about a young boy growing up among them in a local town; the Jewish leaders believed God's Word had been broken.

They imposed presuppositions to the text, and possibly for that, missed their Messiah. Don't do that. Don't force your ideas on the Bible. God sometimes does things a little strange, at least the way we see it. But the prophecy is clear — "Surely the Lord GOD will do nothing, but he revealeth his secret unto his servants the prophets" (Amos 3:7).

Okay, you're a skeptic. Consider another way, as Mark Eastman* notes the following. Luke chapter 3 states Jesus' baptism occurs in the fifteenth year of Tiberius. Tiberius's reign began on August 19 14 AD, so Jesus' first Passover would have been spring AD 29. Most believe Jesus' ministry was 3 ½ years, so the fourth would have been 32 AD. And in 32 AD, the Sunday before Passover that year was April 6, 32 AD, the same day given to Daniel (what a coincidence!).

So that's verse 25. So far it's been simple. But once you arrive, what happens?

The Messiah

> *And after threescore and two weeks shall Messiah be cut off, but not for himself* Daniel 9:26a

After sixty-two weeks is the same as after the sixty-nine weeks (as it's 7 + 62). After that period the Messiah shall be cut off

---
* http://blueletterbible.org/Comm/mark_eastman/messiah/sfm_06.html

(which means executed). But not for Himself (substitution); of course Jesus Himself was innocent, He paid the price for *my* sin, not His (He was sinless), as Chuck Missler examines the gospel according to Barabbas: *

> *The substitution of Barabbas over Jesus before Pilate on that fateful day has profound implications for each of us. It is illuminating to examine the contrast between the two accused more closely:*
>
> - *Barabbas stood under the righteous condemnation of the law.*
> - *Barabbas knew the One who was to take his cross and take his place was innocent.*
> - *Barabbas knew that Jesus Christ was for him a true substitute.*
> - *Barabbas knew that he had done nothing to merit going free while another took his place.*
> - *Barabbas knew Christ's death was for him perfectly efficacious.*
> - *Barabbas and Jesus changed places!* "*The murderer's bonds, curse, disgrace, and mortal agony were transferred to the righteous Jesus; while the liberty, innocence, safety, and well-being of the immaculate Nazarene became the lot of the murderer.*"

The Interval

> *and the people of the prince that shall come shall destroy the city and the sanctuary; and the end thereof shall be with a flood, and unto the end of the war desolations are determined.*
>
> Daniel 9:26b

How do we know an interval exists between 69th and 70th week? Carefully read the passage again, "the people of the prince who is to come shall destroy the city and the sanctuary." The prince who is to come refers to Antichrist, and his people (the Romans) destroyed Jerusalem in 70 AD as a historical event. We know by history the interval lasts at least from 32 AD to 70 AD, and by real experience it's been over 2,000 years.

But the 70th week draws near.

Back to what we started with, this passage concerns the Jews, not the church. What happens in the 70th week? You'll discover in

---

* http://www.khouse.org/articles/2000/217/

Revelation chapters 6–19, but notice what Daniel says regarding the 70th week.

The 70th Week

> And he shall confirm the covenant with many for one week; and in the midst of the week he shall cause the sacrifice and the oblation to cease, and for the overspreading of abominations he shall make it desolate, even until the consummation, and that determined shall be poured upon the desolate.   Daniel 9:27

He is "the prince who is to come," the Antichrist. He shall enforce an agreement with Israel (whether he makes the agreement itself is debatable), but in the middle of the period he breaks the covenant, committing the abomination which causes desolation — it's then the Jews realize their mistake; Revelation expands on the 70th week if you're interested.

> And of the children of Issachar, who were men that had understanding of the times, to know what Israel ought to do;
> 1 Chronicles 12:32

23.4 Didactic and Dialectic Thought

Much of what exists in the "scholarship" arena turns out to be pseudo-scholarship — those with PhD's and other titles claiming to be knowledgeable, yet making basic errors in deduction, reason and logic. Many of those "scholars" make absurd errors, all while sounding scholarly. One reason for those errors stems from didactic verses dialectic thought. Stay with us for a bit as we discuss some terms, but you'll quickly see how these conflicting ideas cause considerable problems for the church, as well as the world at large.

- Didactic analysis involves facts and deduction. It's what most people understand to be logic.
- Dialectic analysis involves consensus and discussion to arrive at a conclusion.

If you're older than 30 or so, you've grown up with didactic thought — analyzing a set of facts to draw a conclusion. Different people may disagree on the conclusions or analysis, but facts are facts, and definitions don't change.

If you've been recently educated (you're younger than 30 or so), you're likely trained in dialectic thinking — using discussion and group-think (even if it's a small group) to arrive at conclusions. Facts may or may not be used, and definitions and concepts shift as required to fit the conclusion.

A similar occurrence happens with atheists — by definition, atheism claims there is no god. Of course, that makes no sense as the only way you can claim there is no god is if you have all knowledge, thus atheism becomes trapped by absurdity.

We're seeing many people calling themselves atheists actually use the term in an agnostic way — agnostics don't have a reason to believe in god, or say we can't know, or no evidence exists, while the atheist makes the bold assertion no god exists. Again, dialectic thinking rescues the illogical position of the atheist, who subtly shifts definitions to suit their purposes. After all, the dialectic atheist says, if other atheists misuse the term that way (discussion and what the group thinks), it must be acceptable.

Terms must be defined — what defines an agnostic, and what defines an atheist? From Websters New World College Dictionary:*

- *athe-ist (n.) A person who believes that there is no God.*

- *ag-nos-tic (n.) A person who believes that the human mind cannot know whether there is a God or an ultimate cause, or anything beyond material phenomena.*

An atheist rejects religious belief and denies the existence of God; an agnostic questions the existence of God, heaven, etc in the absence of material proof and an unwillingness to accept supernatural revelation.

Other dictionaries express similar definitions — "One who believes that there is no deity" (Merriam-Webster), "One who disbelieves or denies the existence of God or gods" (American Heritage), and "a person who denies or disbelieves the existence of a supreme being or beings" (Random House).

The atheist states there is no god, while the agnostic doesn't have a reason to believe, as they see no evidence for god. If atheism equates to agnosticism, why do two words exist with different roots? Only dialectic thought can equate the two and rescue the atheist from the absurdity of his position. Let's take a brief look at some atheist "logic" and you'll quickly notice the dialectic group-think behind the absurdities.

---

* Agnes (2007)

> *The dictionary defines intolerance as lack of toleration, an unwillingness or refusal to tolerate or respect. Sometimes, though, it becomes quite necessary. Intolerance toward beliefs and doctrines that serve only to promote hatred, bigotry and discrimination should be lauded, as should extremist points of view toward the eradication of these beliefs and doctrines.**

He's actually trying to make the laughable, wonderfully logically absurd statement intolerance should be eliminated ... except if it's *his* intolerance, in which case it's not only good, but everyone else should join his extremist intolerance. Naturally, any one with an open mind not clouded by a specific belief dogma immediately notices the absurdity.

Young people (about 30 years old and younger, or those spending extensive time in education, especially in English, history, philosophy, psychology, or similar) have been trained in the dialectic thought process — building consensus, agreement, ignoring facts when needed, shifting definitions, and so on. Very few individuals recently educated understand how to draw conclusions from a set of facts the way their previous generation did. Instead, it's group-think, value relativism, and shifting terms as needed as dialectic thought becomes more common, and absolutes are abandoned.

Of course, dialectic thought equally infects the church, as Christian terms such as Jesus, resurrection, hell, and even Satan change in dialectic tactics to change Christianity from standing for something, to something that falls for anything. How many different winds of doctrine blow through the Church? From the Emergent Church to social justice, they all have one thing in common — using dialectic thought to change meaning, either to better meld with the world and its views, or to avoid those pesky areas of the Bible remaining stubbornly clear.

It might surprise you to learn some pastors don't hold to the virgin birth, reality of hell, existence of Satan, inerrancy of the Bible, the rapture, literal return of Jesus, and many other basic Christian doctrines. They may sound orthodox — even using the same terms — but they don't mean the same as they use dialectic thought.

The question for the church is simple — when did God's Word become insufficient? When did it become irrelevant? And why

---

* http://atheists.org/blog/2011/09/14/taking-the-gloves-off (accessed Nov 12, 2011)

abandon the absolute of God's Word for the shifting sand of man's wisdom?

Your first task in your study is learning (or re-learning) true logical thought. Once you understand the basics, you'll be *stunned* to notice how often so-called smart people commit staggering errors in logic.

23.5 Post-Modern Philosophy

POST-MODERNISM DENIES ABSOLUTE truth (perhaps you've heard the slogan "that's truth for *you*"). Post-modern philosophy embraces experience and feelings over reason and logic, group-think and consensus instead of truth. Truth becomes relative and not absolute — some actually proclaim no absolute truth exists — an idea they proclaim absolutely (as the only absolute truth), demonstrating how circular and illogical their thought process is.

Post-modernism employs the dialectic process, using group-think and consensus to arrive at "truth." If you think that's not a good idea, you're correct, as for most people the thought of negotiating what 2+2 equals sounds bizarre (it doesn't just sound bizarre, it *is*). How does this work in practice? Consider the following strange definition of sin.

> *From time to time, I have been asked in the academic classrooms where I have taught to define what I mean by sin. I always respond by saying, "Sin is what diminishes the humanity of another person and of the self."**

Suppose you told someone they were living contrary to God's law (adultery, drunkenness, etc). According to the previous definition of sin a Christian speaking truth sins, as it has the possibility to make the person feel sad. Boo hoo hoo. Send a Hallmark card instead.

Remember David when he murdered one of his men? What did he say to God in Psalm 51 — "Against thee, thee only, have I sinned, and done this evil in thy sight." No mention of "dehumanizing," the offense is *always* against God, even if effects are felt here on earth.

Redefining sin removes God from the equation, reducing sin to whatever you want it to be — it's not constant, but whatever

---

*   http://www.redletterchristians.org/what-do-you-mean-by-sin/

"diminishes the humanity" of a person. Not only is God not involved, but neither is *truth*. If speaking the truth bums someone out, that's sin on your part. Yet sin is against God — it's not about dehumanizing another person or yourself. Those may be *results* of sin, but they're most definitely not the *definition* of sin.

Where is the absolute inerrant Word of God? Nowhere to be found — only whatever man decides. A perfect example of post-modern value relativism, and the removal of God from what they call "Christianity" — reducing Christianity to a man-centered philosophy changing day to day.

I can hear you now; that's an isolated case, it doesn't happen that often. Really? Consider the fad of "social justice" sweeping through the church in the early 2000s. You'll quickly discover social justice contains nothing more than repackaged post-modern philosophy. First off, we need to define terms. What is social justice?

> *Social justice is based on the concepts of human rights and equality and involves a greater degree of economic egalitarianism through progressive taxation, income redistribution, or even property redistribution.**
>
> *Economic egalitarianism is a state of economic affairs in which equality of outcome has been manufactured for all the participants of a society. It is a founding principle of various forms of socialism, communalism and cooperative economic organization.*†

In short, social justice attempts to manufacture a society with everyone having equal amounts of property, money, and everything else. Specifically, it's not equality of *opportunity* they seek (a fair and level playing field), it's equality of *outcome* — an outcome forced by confiscation and redistribution if needed. If you think that sounds like Marx's "from each according to his ability, to each according to his needs" you're quite correct.

As a political idea, you might agree or disagree with it — that's fine. However, when someone claims Christians should support such an idea as your Christian duty, ask them where Jesus or any New Testament author claimed the church should lobby for

---

* http://en.wikipedia.org/wiki/Social_justice (accessed Nov 12, 2011, though Wikipedia changes a lot.)

† http://en.wikipedia.org/wiki/Economic_egalitarianism (accessed Nov 12, 2011, though Wikipedia changes a lot.)

forced confiscation of a person's income or property for the sole purpose of redistribution and equality of outcome (not fairness). You'll get a deer-in-the-headlights look, because they *know* it's not there, yet in their next breath they'll tell you it's your Christian duty to support it anyway. Tilt.

Some even go so far as to change the definition of the Gospel to include redistributive ideas — another case where post-modern philosophy runs straight into conflict with the Bible, as Paul exactly defines the Gospel.

> *Moreover, brethren, I declare unto you the gospel which I preached unto you ... For I delivered unto you first of all that which I also received, how that Christ died for our sins according to the scriptures; And that he was buried, and that he rose again the third day according to the scriptures...* 1 Corinthians 15

Strange. No mention of social justice in any form at all. How can it be integral to the Gospel? It's not, as those people aren't using the Biblical definition of the Gospel, they're using some alternate gospel and not telling you about it. Recall Paul's warning about alternate gospels.

> *But though we, or an angel from heaven, preach any other gospel unto you than that which we have preached unto you, let him be accursed. As we said before, so say I now again, If any man preach any other gospel unto you than that ye have received, let him be accursed. For do I now seek the favor of men, or God? Or do I seek to please men? For if I yet pleased men, I should not be the servant of Christ. But I make known to you, brethren, that the gospel which was preached of me is not after man.* Galatians 1:8-11

According to Paul, where should post-modern philosophical ideas changing Biblical definitions end up? On the scrap heap. It's left to the reader to examine each idea and question the person asking *why* they're abandoning the Bible, and what they want to replace it with. They'll be slippery about it of course, but force them to define terms, and you'll discover some people use the same words but with totally different meanings.

You need to understand post-modern philosophy because new fads in the church use post-modern thought as those groups seek to redefine the Bible to suit whatever purpose they're actually trying to achieve — whatever that purpose may be, it certainly isn't Christianity. As post-modern philosophy infects the church, you must be able to recognize bizarre non-Biblical ideas for what they are — lies, distortions, heresy, and a denial of God's absolute Word. And we state that absolutely, in spite of post-modernism claiming absolute truth doesn't exist.

Post-modern philosophy and the denial of absolute truth allows heretics to creep into the church and deceive many. They will *never* identify themselves as such ("hi, I'm a heretic and I'm here to move you away from God's Word"), and will even use normal Christian words such as sin, justice, redemption, hell, salvation, and more, but their ideas remain in conflict with the Bible, and you'll notice a subtle shift (sometimes not even subtle) away from God's inerrant Word towards whatever ideas they want to replace the Bible with.

23.6 The Problem of Evil

Christians eventually run into problems and questions requiring an answer. You might encounter skeptics and others posing questions they believe require an answer denying the existence of God. They'll even try and place you into a position appearing to offer no other solution than admitting God either doesn't exist, or can't possibly posses the characteristics the Bible states He has.

The existence of evil remains such a question; the problem is those posing the question don't actually understand the nature of what they're asking; since God created Satan this implies God created evil. How can a pure, good, and loving god create evil? If God is good, and God is righteous, why did God create evil? Does this make Him not good, or evil Himself?

The question presupposes evil exists as a quantifiable entity. We're not saying evil forces don't exist, but we'll need a bit of background before we arrive at the answer. Don't make the error evil doesn't exist, as it most certainly does; those seeking to deny it become trapped in their own delusions.

First, think of hot and cold — do they exist? Well, yes and no. Heat does exist, but cold doesn't, as the absence of heat defines cold. Cold as a physical quantity does not exist — what you experience isn't cold, but a lack of heat.

That may sound like splitting hairs on a definition, but it's crucial. You see, if cold existed as a quantity, absolute zero would not exist (absolute zero being the lowest possible temperature, roughly -273 Celsius, or -460 Fahrenheit). If cold existed as a physical quantity, by continually adding cold no lower bound of temperature would exist.

Thus, heat exists, cold doesn't — it's only the absence of heat.

Consider light and dark. Similar to cold, darkness doesn't exist. If you've ever been in a cave or other completely dark situation, you know once it's totally black, it can't get darker — you've removed all the light, and what's left is darkness. You can't add "darkness" to make it blacker, all you can do is remove all the light.

So back to our original question — did God create evil? The answer should be obviously no — the Bible says all creation was good, it later became evil. How did that happen? By ceasing to be good, Satan became evil. It's not a quantity of evil added, it's the removal (or rejection) of good creating evil. "Pure" evil therefore, is the removal of all goodness, not a creation of God — it's a choice of His creation.

Evil isn't a real quantity, but evil forces do exist as they have chosen to reject God's goodness, but God didn't create evil.

23.7 That's Not What I Meant!

Ever notice things don't often work out the way you want? Me too. Most people wonder why their plans don't work out — after all, we've been praying for years, why isn't God answering? I've got good ideas here, Lord, why don't you try this? Why isn't God doing something? Anything? Where is the abundant life Jesus promised?

A prophet in the Bible had the same problem: Habakkuk.

> *The burden which Habakkuk the prophet did see. O Lord, how long shall I cry, and thou wilt not hear! Even cry out unto thee of violence, and thou wilt not save! Why dost thou show me iniquity, and cause me to behold grievance? For spoiling and violence are before me; and there are that raise up strife and contention. Therefore the law is slacked, and justice doth never go forth; for the wicked doth compass about the righteous; therefore justice goeth forth perverted.* Habakkuk 1:1-4

Habakkuk looks around his country and sees violence, a lack of justice, and a lack of following God's law. Sounds familiar, huh? Take a look around our country and we see the same thing — wickedness, violence and an utter contempt for the Word of God. Like anyone in that position, what he sees disturbs him, praying to God for the country to turn around. I'm sure Habakkuk had great ideas in mind, but God answers Habakkuk with a plan probably not on his mind as he prayed for God to intercede.

> *Behold ye among the nations, and regard, and wonder marvelously; for I will work a work in your days, which ye will not believe, though it be told you. For, lo, I raise up the Chaldeans, that bitter and hasty nation, which shall march through the breadth of the land, to possess the dwelling places that are not theirs.* Habakkuk 1:5-6

God plans to use the enemy of Israel as His arm of judgment. This happened many times in Israel's history, so it's not unusual, but using the brutal Chaldeans causes Habakkuk some confusion.

> *Thou art of purer eyes than to behold evil, and canst not look on iniquity; why lookest thou upon them that deal treacherously, and holdest thy tongue when the wicked devoureth the man that is more righteous than he?* Habakkuk 1:13

Habakkuk's short response — that's not what I meant! How can you let those evil people take over the land? We're not that bad, Lord. Yes, I've been praying for the nation, and I see nothing but evil around, but you've got to be kidding Lord! The Chaldeans? I didn't have that in mind — I was thinking more of a revival or a great spiritual movement. Not the Chaldeans Lord!

And thus the problem. We ask God to intercede but then provide conditions and stipulations on His actions; God doesn't work that way. When you ask the creator of the universe to intercede on your behalf, you must allow Him room to work — He has more knowledge than you do. Don't go it your own way with disaster looming large ahead, like a giant iceberg waiting for your ship to sail by.

You can't ask God to intervene and then try and force your plan on Him. It just won't work because you don't have the same knowledge He has. Suppose your job isn't so great and God has this great new job for you and is just waiting for you to trust in Him for it. But you don't (or won't), so you get laid off. You see, God had a new job for you all along, but you weren't looking for it.

Now you are.

What would be the natural response? O God, why me? I know it wasn't the best job, but it paid the bills. How will I feed my family now? Instead of trusting in God, we pout and complain. That's not what I meant Lord! (which defines oxymoron — words that don't go together. You can't say "Not so, Lord"). I wanted life to be easy. But God isn't concerned with easy, He's concerned about character. And *character matters.*

God sees the end from the beginning and knows what's best for us. Just as we teach a child, the Lord wants to teach us. Just as the child pouts and complains when things don't go their way, so do we. But the difference is the two-year-old doesn't have the capacity to understand what's going on. We should.

One problem remains — if we trust in God, how do we know He's going to take care of us?

> *And we know that all things work together for good to them that love God, to them who are the called according to his purpose.*
> Romans 8:28)

> *For I know the thoughts that I think toward you, saith the LORD, thoughts of peace, and not of evil, to give you an expected end.*
> Jeremiah 29:11

Notice one thing: We are never guaranteed understanding. That's what we really want, but won't get. That's where trust in the Lord comes in. It's easy to trust when you see the plan, but what about when you don't? Is it really trust if you can see it? Nope. It's only trust when you don't understand and can't see.

> *I have been young, and now am old; yet have I not seen the righteous forsaken, nor his seed begging bread.* Psalm 37:25

What must we do? Habakkuk had the answer for his problem, and it's the same answer for us.

> *I will stand upon my watch, and set me upon the tower, and will watch to see what he will say unto me, and what I shall answer when I am reproved.* Habakkuk 2:1

Wait on the Lord, but don't wait for understanding. You want the peace that passes understanding, not the peace from understanding. Allow God to work. As the saying goes "don't just do something, stand there."

CHAPTER XXIV

Conclusion

Now you should be ready to *begin* serious training — the black belt isn't the end, it's the beginning. It's the *minimum* required, but never the end. Do you have a goal for your progress? Or just a dream?

Understand if you're discouraged right now, the message coming from Zechariah and Haggai remains as relevant today as it was then — it's time to get back in the game, for the end is sure. You may not *feel* victorious currently, but in God's frame of reference the deal is done, and the victory has already been obtained.

Your progress may be fast or slow, so don't measure yourself against others, but write it down, set a goal, get it done, and get back in the game.

Because at 3 AM you've got what you've got ... it's 2:59 AM ... and you're *not* Chuck Norris.

It was character that got us out of bed, commitment that moved us into action, and discipline that enabled us to follow through.
~ Zig Ziglar

References

Agnes, M. (Ed.) (2007). *Webster's New World College Dictionary* (4 ed.). Wiley Publishing, Inc.

Courson, J. (2006). *Jon Courson's Application Commentary, Old Testament*, Volume II. Thomas Nelson.

Feynman, R. (1964). *The Feynman Lectures on Physics*, Volume I. Addison-Wesley.

Lewis, C. (1990). *The Screwtape Letters*. Barbour and Company.

Lucado, M. (2005). *Thomas Nelson*. Thomas Nelson.

McGee, J. V. (1982). *Thru the Bible*, Volume III. Thomas Nelson.

Sewell, M. (2009). The Hitchens Transcript. *Portland Monthly* http://www.portlandmonthlymag.com/arts-and-entertainment/category/books-and-talks/articles/christopher-hitchens/. Accessed 2012-07-16.

Taunton, L. (2007, 12). Richard Dawkins: The Atheist Evangelist. *byFaith* http://byfaithonline.com/richard-dawkins-the-atheist-evangelist/. Accessed 2012-07-19.

www.ingramcontent.com/pod-product-compliance
Lightning Source LLC
LaVergne TN
LVHW041939070526
838199LV00051BA/2844